D1436202

Picture Source Book
for Social History

LATE NINETEENTH CENTURY

Picture Source Book
for Social History

FROM THE CONQUEST TO THE WARS OF THE ROSES
by Molly Harrison & A. A. M. Wells, M.A.

SIXTEENTH CENTURY
by Molly Harrison & Margaret E. Bryant, M.A.

(Second Impression)

SEVENTEENTH CENTURY
by Molly Harrison & A. A. M. Wells, M.A.

"The pictures are well chosen and worthy of a delightful book which we cordially recommend."—*Journal of Education*

"This unusually useful book . . ."—*Times Educational Supplement*

EIGHTEENTH CENTURY
by Molly Harrison & A. A. M. Wells, M.A.

"This is a provocative book in the best sense; one begins by dipping into it and before long one is submerged."—*Journal of Education*

". . . a most elegant volume."—*Times Educational Supplement*

EARLY NINETEENTH CENTURY
by Molly Harrison & A. A. M. Wells, M.A.

Picture Source Book
for Social History

LATE NINETEENTH CENTURY

BY

MOLLY HARRISON
Curator, the Geffrye Museum

AND

O. M. ROYSTON
B.A.

London
GEORGE ALLEN & UNWIN LTD
RUSKIN HOUSE MUSEUM STREET

ACKNOWLEDGMENTS

The provenance of the pictures is gratefully acknowledged to Aerofilms, Figs. 31, 50; Birmingham Museum and Art Gallery, Fig. 36; Castle Museum, York, Fig. 7; Harris Art Gallery, Preston, Figs. 4, 8, 9, 72; Illustrated London News, Figs. 32, 33, 44, 96; The London Museum, Fig. 27; Mansell Collection, Fig. 88; William Morris Gallery, Fig. 21; National Buildings Record, Figs. 9, 56, 57, 58, 59, 60, 62; National Maritime Museum, Fig. 48; Proprietors of Punch, Figs. 23, 34, 35; Radio Times Hulton Picture Library, Figs. 3, 5, 6, 28, 29, 39, 43, 64, 73, 74, 80, 81, 82, 83, 84, 85; Royal Holloway College, Fig. 42; Royal Institute of British Architects, Fig. 52; The Shaftesbury Society, Fig. 86; Trustees of the Tate Gallery, Fig. 2; Victoria and Albert Museum, Figs. 10, 14, 15, 16, 17, 18, 20; Frederick Warne & Co., Ltd., Fig. 25; Wellcome Historical Medical Museum, Figs. 91, 92. The Tenniel drawing on the title page is reproduced by permission of Macmillan & Co., Ltd.

The following extracts are reproduced from Punch: Nos. 1–5, 16, 25, 32–3, 37, 51, 59, 68, 71, 76, 83, 85–7, 91, 109, 119.

AUTHOR'S NOTE

As Curator of a London County Council Museum, I am required to state that the Council is in no way responsible for the views expressed in this book

PRINTED IN GREAT BRITAIN
in Baskerville type
BY UNWIN BROTHERS LIMITED, WOKING AND LONDON

Read This First

Queen Victoria reigned longer than any other English monarch. She came to the throne as a young girl in 1837 and died, a tired, lonely old lady, in 1901. So the second half of the nineteenth century, the subject of this book, was all Victorian.

We nowadays often think of the Victorians as stuffy, prim and rather dull people. Family feeling was very strong; father was very much the head of the household and mother, the children and the servants obeyed him without question. People kept their place in their own class, too, and were not nearly so free or natural as they can be today.

Yet this was a most adventurous age. People's ideas and beliefs as well as the things they made and used and the way they lived, were changing rapidly.

Britain, together with her overseas Empire, was becoming the leading country of the world. As a nation, our trade and industry were making us prosperous. Yet there were still a great many poor people living in dreadful conditions, so that Disraeli, the great Conservative Prime Minister, rightly described England as being "two nations"—rich and poor. Much was being done, however, to improve matters. Many writers, statesmen and philanthropists were deeply concerned and the workers in the cities, too, were struggling to improve their own conditions, so that gradually some of the worst injustices were abolished. Above all, everybody believed in progress. However bad conditions were, English men and women knew that things had been worse in the early years of the century and were convinced that they would go on improving.

This was a time when appearances mattered a great deal and yet during the nineteenth century more ugly things were made and used than ever before. The industrial cities spread rapidly and without any proper planning, so that a blight of ugly, mean streets spread where countryside and village had been before. For the wealthy, ostentation mattered more than elegance and many of the things they liked seem to us to be vulgar and over-decorated.

We know about this period in greater detail than we know about any earlier periods. For one thing, there are people still living who remember those days and who like to talk about when they were young. If you have any relatives or friends who are more than seventy years old you will find it interesting to ask if they can tell you about anything mentioned in this book which they themselves saw or heard about.

More and more people were learning to read and more and more newspapers were reporting details of events both at home and abroad. They were not like our newspapers, for they had few headlines and hardly any pictures, but they do give us plenty of first-hand evidence about life during the later nineteenth century. The most varied and interesting of the newspapers from that point of view is *Punch* which, week by week, poked fun at new fashions, customs and ideas. Without Mr. Punch we should know a great deal less than we do about our Victorian forefathers.

Photography had been invented before 1850, but only gradually did it come to be widely used. Notice which of our illustrations are reproductions of photographs, which are of drawings and which are of paintings.

Partly because things were changing so rapidly and because the Queen's reign had spanned so long a period, many people were interested in looking back and in writing of what they remembered. "Memoirs" were of course written mainly by well-to-do people who had both education and leisure. Not only do they tell us about people and their doings, but the language of many of them is also revealing. The style is pompous and rather heavy. Victorians were conscious of their dignity and cared a great deal about appearances and reputation. They never dreamt of being familiar or easy-going in public, whether in their actions or in their writings. If you read carefully you will probably be able to decide which of the extracts come from books written before 1900 and which are from more recent writings, where the authors have looked back from their twentieth-century selves, at their nineteenth-century youth.

We have not changed any of the wording at all. The English language has not altered very much during the past hundred years, though the phrases have become shorter, quicker and less rolling, as you would expect.

Do remember that this is not a story book—it is not meant to be read right through; it is a *reference* book, for you to dip into when you want an idea or a piece of information. This means that a very important part of the book is the INDEX, which tells you which page to go to in order to find what you want. Because we think the index is especially important in this book we have put it first, and not at the back as is usual.

Nursery rhymes illustrated by Kate Greenaway and *Alice in Wonderland* (see title page) were popular books for children.

CONTENTS

The design on the binding of this volume is taken from the first book printed by William Morris's Kelmscott Press.

INDEX

The numbers in italics refer to the pictures. The ordinary numbers refer to the text (the extracts and the comments on them).

1. Fashions for girls in 1866. Imagine how long it took them to dress and how carefully they had to move

3. City fashions, shown in *The West End Gazette* of June 1880

2. A painting of 1852. Notice the hair style, hats, an artificial flower under a glass dome

4. A photograph from a family album, 1860. Notice the little girl's long "pantalettes"

5. Walking in Hyde Park in the 1870s

6. An evening at home in the 1860s

7. A Victorian parlour. Notice ornaments, pictures and patterned surfaces

8. A bouquet holder, for flowers to be worn on the dress

9. Victorian mantelpieces held many curious vases and ornaments. That on the left is called a "lustre" because of the reflection from the glass pendants

10. Pottery designed by William de Morgan in 1890. Compare with pottery in Nos. 7 and 8

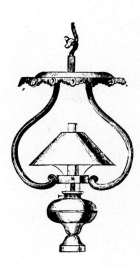

11 and 12. Oil lamps, shown at the Great Exhibition, 1851. These gave a much better light than candles

13. Did you think that glass drop-down oven doors and a spit attachment were modern ideas? This gas cooker was in use in 1890

14. A chair made of papiermâché

15. Sideboard by James Wilcox. Notice the elaborate carving

16. Cabinet in oak, with brass panels, by A. W. Pugin, 1851. Notice the medieval type of carving

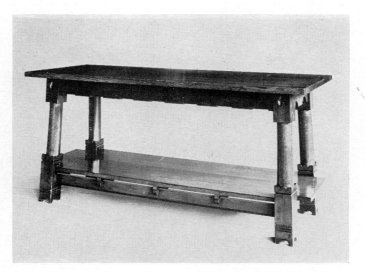

17. Table designed by Philip Webb, about 1870

18. Furniture designed by E. W. Godwin, about 1870. Compare these with the elaborate furniture on the previous page

19. Children's toys: a swing boat and a doll in the costume of 1872

20. Wallpaper designed by Bruce Talbert, 1877

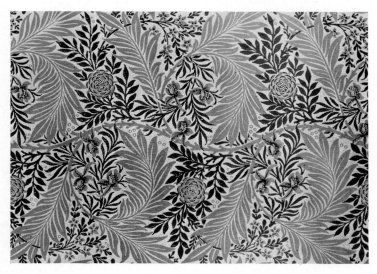

21. "Larkspur" wallpaper designed by William Morris, 1872. Compare
both these with the wallpaper in No. 7

23

22. Boys learning tailoring at a school for truants, 1893

23. Girls at boarding school out for a walk, 1876

24. Prayers at a church school in 1892. Notice pinafores, boots and long desks

25. Lucy Locket: an illustration in a book of nursery
rhymes, drawn by Kate Greenaway

26. London street urchins, 1899

26

27. A summer's day in Hyde Park. In how many different ways are people enjoying themselves?

28. Fishing in 1890

29. Archery was a favourite sport for women, 1885

28

30. Skating in the park, 1885

31. Playing bowls in 1878

32. A cross-country run in 1869

33. Gymnastics in 1888. How much of this apparatus do you still use?

34. At the seaside. A cartoon from *Punch*. Do you know how the bathing machine was used?

35. Tennis in 1883

31

36. "A Railway Journey," painted by W. S. Frith. Third-class carriages had a roof by this time, but no sides

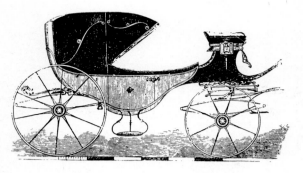

37. A barouche shown at the Great Exhibition

38. Another carriage shown at the Exhibition

39. A "knifeboard" omnibus in 1868. Up to ten passengers were
allowed to travel on the top. Notice the very tall hats

40. Thomson's "road steamer" at Edinburgh in 1870

41. A railway disaster at Kentish Town in 1861

34

42. Paddington Station in 1862, painted by W. S. Frith. Notice luggage being stacked on the roof

43. London's first tramway, opened in 1861

44. Horse buses racing a steam bus along a London street in 1898

45. Outside Charing Cross Station. Can you find a hansom cab and a hackney carriage?

46. Cycling in 1896

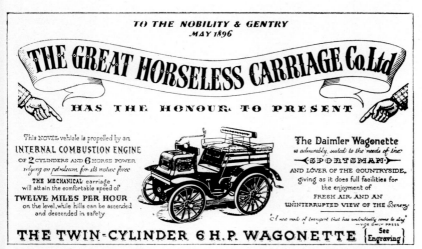

47. An advertisement for a new kind of vehicle. Notice to whom the notice is addressed and when. How fast could the vehicle travel?

48. Tea clippers racing home from the East. The *Ariel* and the *Taeping* off the Lizard in 1866

49. An iron steamboat. The Union Company's S.S. *Trojan* in 1880

50. The opening of Tower Bridge, June 30, 1894

51. Gas Company's Offices in Sheffield, built in 1879 in the "early Renaissance" style

52. The Great Hall at Euston Station, London, designed as a dramatic beginning to the adventure of travelling by railway

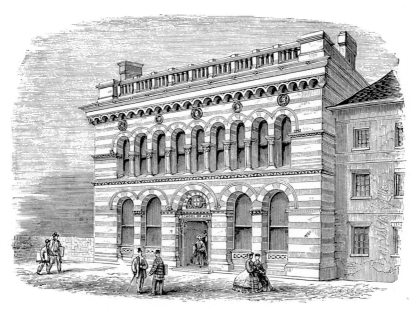

53. The School of Art, Sheffield, built in 1880 to look like an Italian Palace

54. Merryweather's carriage fire-engine, "to be drawn by two or four horses," 1851. How do you think water was pumped on to a burning building?

55. A developing industrial town. Sheffield in 1879. Notice the horse-drawn tram

56. Kelham Hall, Nottinghamshire, designed by Sir Gilbert Scott. Notice the "Gothic" details: pointed windows, an oriel window, battlements, turrets and a spire

58. Northampton Town Hall, designed by E. W. Godwin in the "medieval" style, 1864. A great many Town Halls were built after the Municipal Corporations Act of 1860

57. The Law Courts, London, designed by G. E. Street. This was the last great building in the "Victorian Gothic" style

60. Whitfield Street School, London, by E. R. Robson. A very modern building in 1880, designed in the "Queen Anne" style

59. All Saint's Church, Margaret Street, London, W.1, designed by William Butterfield in 1859. Both inside and out the surfaces are decorated in multi-coloured brick

62. Model dwellings for poor families, 1850

61. Slum houses in 1899

45

64. Playing in a London street in 1892

63. Police inspecting vagrants with a bull's-eye lantern in 1872.
An etching by Gustav Doré

46

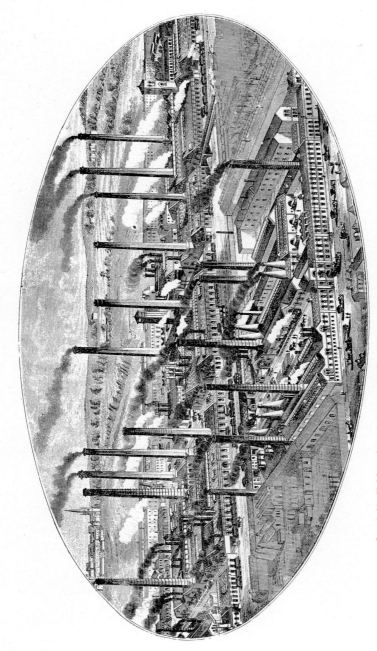

65. A Sheffield steel works in the middle of the century. Notice how close the countryside still is

66. Inside a steel works

67. Rolling armour-plated steel. Notice hand pulling by twelve men

68. A match factory in 1870. Notice how many of the processes were carried out by hand

69. A reaping machine shown at the Great Exhibition. Previously all reaping had been by hand

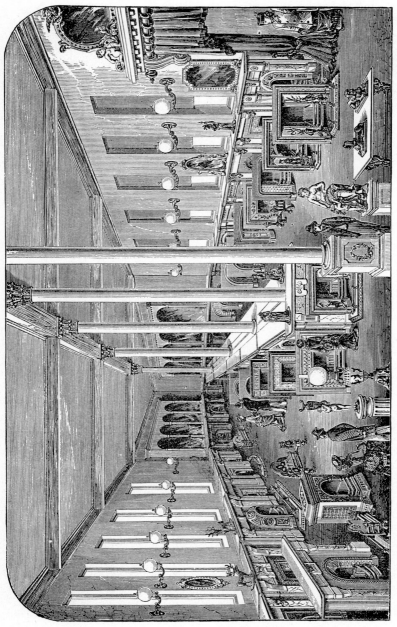

70. A showroom for coal-burning grates. Notice the size and decoration of the grates and the lighting of the showroom

51

MAPPIN AND WEBB'S

ELECTRO-PLATE
OF THE FINEST QUALITY.

MAPPIN
AND
WEBB'S

REGISTERED
"EDINBOROUGH"
GUARD FORK.

SHOW ROOMS AND MANUFACTORY:
NORFOLK STREET,
SHEFFIELD.

MAPPIN & WEBB'S
Patent "Club" Bottle Holder
The simplest and best ever invented.

ILLUSTRATED CATALOGUES Post Free.

MAPPIN & WEBB,
NORFOLK STREET, SHEFFIELD;
AND
LONDON SHOW ROOMS,

OPEN.

CLOSED.

76, 77 & 78, OXFORD STREET, W., & MANSION HOUSE BUILDINGS, CITY.

71. Advertising the new process of electro-plating, which made cheaper metals look
like silver. Compare this advertisement with our style of newspaper advertising

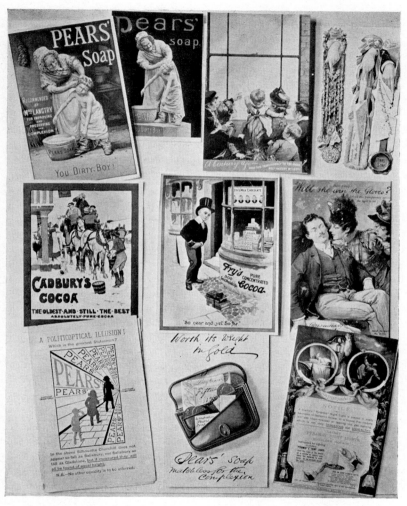

72. Some examples of advertising of the period. Perhaps you can compare these with Pears', Cadbury's and Fry's advertisements today. Notice (bottom line) that gold coins were still in circulation

73. A new machine advertised in 1885. It cost 8 guineas

74. By 1900 the first electricity power stations were being built. They were then as revolutionary as atomic power stations are today

75. A photograph of the front of the Great Exhibition in Hyde Park, taken on the opening day, May 1, 1851. Photography was then something quite new

76. Prince Albert being cheered by workmen when he visited the Exhibition site. The dray is bringing beer for the workmen

77. The galleries of the Exhibition were tested for safety by rolling weights on the floors, by stamping workmen and by marching troops

78. The main entrance

79. The main gallery. These two pictures are not photographs but drawings. Notice how trees were not cut down but left inside the great exhibition halls

80. Gold mining in Western Australia in 1857

81. A sketch by H. M. Stanley of an Englishman meeting an African tribe

82. The Indian Mutiny at Lucknow, July 1857. After its suppression Victoria was proclaimed Empress of India. Previously the government had still been partly in the hands of the East India Company

83. Battle of Sebastopol

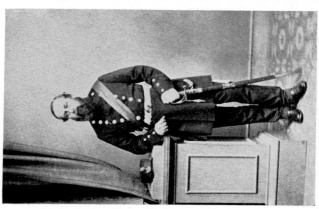

84. Officers' uniforms. Soldiers were still known as "Redcoats." It was not until the Boer War, 1899–1901, that uniforms were changed to dull khaki to prevent the soldiers showing up against their background

85. H.M.S. *Devastation*, 1872. Notice the "crow's nest." Do you know its purpose?

86. Orphan boys in training for the Navy on the first *Arethusa*, 1880. This was one of the charities started by Lord Shaftesbury

87. A fish market in 1870 lit by naked gas jets. Gas mantles, which
gave a much better light, came into use about 1890

88. A Staffordshire coal-mine, also lit by a gas jet. If the "galleries" were
very low, children crawling along on hands and knees were used instead of
pit-ponies

89. Paying out an under-sea telegraph cable from the hold of a ship in 1853

90. The first telephone conversation between London and Paris, March 1891

91. Dr. James Simpson and two friends discover the effect of chloroform in November 1847. Chloroform made it possible to carry out more difficult operations than could be risked while the patient was conscious all the time and had to be held down

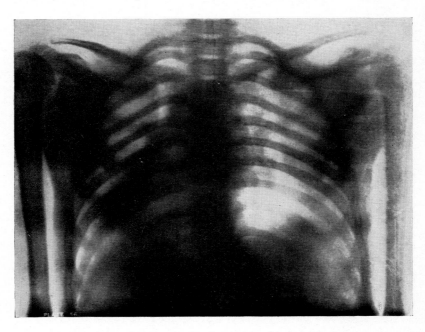

92. An early X-ray photograph by Röntgen, 1897, showing the chest of a boy of fourteen. This was a startling advance as it enabled doctors to see inside the human body

The People and Their Clothes

(See the pictures on pp. 13–16.)

Clothes were of dull, drab colours during much of the second half of the nineteenth century. Queen Victoria's husband, Prince Albert, was a solemn man and his influence was felt in fashion as well as in behaviour. When he died in 1861 Queen Victoria went into mourning; black and purple then became the fashionable colours.

During this period women changed their shape a great deal. During the 1850s and early 1860s it was smart to wear a steel frame, or crinoline, for holding out your skirts.

Punch *commented frequently upon new fashions as they came out. Here is an amusing incident reported in December 1858:*

Visitors to the Cattle Show, at least those who go in Crinoline, would do well, before they start, to read the following short paragraph, which we extract for their perusal from a country print:

"Within a very few minutes of the Show being opened, a distinguished party of ladies and gentlemen arrived, and on coming to the turnstile (which was then the only entrance) it was discovered that the ladies, who we need not say were dressed in all the amplitude of fashion, could not possibly squeeze through so limited a space. In this dilemma, as the turnstile could not possibly be widened to the width that was required, the only course was, obviously, to throw open the great gates, through which the ladies, not without a titter, sailed majestically Show-wards in the wake of the prize beasts." (1)

Accidents were sometimes caused by crinolines. Here is one reported in 1861:

. . . the accidents from Crinolines are, it would seem, upon the increase. Half a score at least have occurred through fire . . . and several others we could cite have taken place from other causes. One of the last we saw reported was occasioned by a dress being caught up by a cab-wheel while the wearer was crossing a street at the West End. Here the victim was so fortunate as to escape with merely a bad fracture of her leg; but in most cases the sufferers have lost their life by their absurdity in wearing the wide dresses which are now accounted fashionable. (2)

Crinolines did not stay in fashion for long. (Can you think of any reasons why, from this time onwards, fashions changed much more quickly than they had done before?)

By 1865 Punch *was complaining about another fashion in ladies' skirts:*

LADIES AND THEIR LONG TAILS

Crinoline at length is going out, thank goodness! but long trailing dresses are coming in, thank badness! In matters of costume lovely woman rarely ceases to make herself a nuisance; and the length of her skirt now is almost as annoying as, a while ago, its width was. Everywhere you walk, your footsteps are impeded by the ladies, who, in Pope's phrase, "drag their slow length along" the pathway just in front of you. "Will anybody tread upon the tail of my petticoat?" This seems to be the general invitation they now give. Sad enemies to progress they are, in their long dresses; and a Reform Bill should be passed to make them hold their tails up. (3)

Long hair was much admired during this period and fashionable ladies paid very great attention to the style of their hairdressing. In the mid 1860s it was smart to wear your hair drawn back into a large "chignon" or bun. If your hair was not long enough to make a large chignon, you could buy false hair to pad it with.

Here are some verses written for a young lady of fashion in the mid 1860s:

I love thee for thy chignon, for the boss of purchased hair,
Which thou hast on thine occiput the charming taste to wear.
Oh, what a grace that ornament unto thy poll doth lend,
Wound on what seems a curtain-rod with knobs at either end!

I love thee for the roses, purchased too, thy cheeks that deck,
The lilies likewise that adorn thy pearly-powdered neck,
And all that sweet "illusion" that, o'er thy features spread,
Improves the poor reality of Nature's white and red.

I love thee for the muslin and the gauze about thee bound,
Like endive that in salad doth a lobster's tail surround.
And oh! I love thee for the boots thine ankles that protect,
So proper to the manly style young ladies now affect.
    (*The boots were probably stout laced-up "Balmorals."*) (4)

Small waists were much admired too and the narrower your waist the smarter you were thought to be. Women and girls sometimes did themselves much harm by wearing very tight corsets. In 1869 the Morning Post, *a London newspaper, carried a sad paragraph, headed "Tight-Lacing," which reported the particulars of an inquest held at the College Arms, Crowndale Road, Camden Town, London, on the body of a young woman aged only nineteen:*

"She was out three hours with a perambulator, in which was one child, and as she neared her destination she fell down insensible . . . upon examination by Dr. Smellie she was found quite dead. It was discovered that she was very tightly-laced, and Dr. Smellie stated that death was caused by effusion of blood on the brain, caused by fatty heart, accelerated by compression of the chest produced by tight-lacing. . . ."(5)

Babies, too, were tightly bound in a great many clothes:
. . . there were considerably more clothes than there was baby. It had . . . a binder. This was a length of flannel wound round and round its tiny person and fastened by a safety-pin. Sometimes, despite care, that safety pin entered the baby and it protested with good cause. Then garments were put upon it, many garments, little vests, a curious kind of overall, vest and petticoat in one piece, made of flannel and laced up with tape, then more petticoats. And above all this, the glory of "long clothes." Very long clothes indeed, the spotless robes of muslin, crepe de Chine, nainsook and the like, beautifully embroidered or smocked, full of lace and ribbons everywhere. . . . (6)

Everyone wore a great many underclothes:

This is what a young lady wore, with whom I shared a room one night. . . .

1. Thick, long-legged, long-sleeved combinations.
2. Over them, white cotton combinations, with plenty of buttons and frills.
3. Very serious, bony, grey stays, with suspenders.
4. Black woollen stockings.
5. White cotton drawers, with buttons and frills.
6. White cotton petticoat-bodice, with embroidery, buttons and frills.
7. Rather short, white flannel, petticoat.
8. Long alpaca petticoat, with a flounce round the bottom.
9. Pink flannel blouse.
10. High, starched, white collar, fastened on with studs.
11. Navy-blue tie.
12. Blue skirt, touching the ground, and fastened tightly to the blouse with a safety-pin behind.
13. Leather belt, very tight.
14. High button boots.

I watched her under my eyelashes as I lay in bed. She would have been horrified if she had known that I was awake. (7)

But many new ideas and new customs were in the air. Bicycles were coming into use among up-to-date people and a Mrs. Bloomer decided to wear special clothes for when she went riding on her bicycle. Here is a letter written in 1892, which shows what many people thought of the new style of clothing:

Two ladies—or, as Grandpapa says, two shameless females—in bloomers bicycled through the village yesterday, and some of the women were so scandalized that they threw stones at them. I didn't dare to say so but I thought they looked very neat, though I don't think I should like to show my own legs to the world like that. Still, it's all a question of what one is accustomed to. Why do old people always disapprove of anything which they didn't do when they were young? (8)

In country districts life still changed very little and people's clothes lasted a long time. Here is a description of an old village couple in the 1860s. Notice that it was the custom for men and women to sit on opposite sides of the church.

Eli's grandfather did not wear side whiskers, but shaved the regions about his lips, leaving a sandy-grey fringe round his chin. Being somewhat old-fashioned in his tastes, he clung to the garb of his youth—corduroy trousers, and the picturesque smock-frock made of greyish linen worked in white or blue thread, completing his costume with a red neck handkerchief, and a shaggy top-hat for Sundays. Thus dressed he attended morning service except during the lambing season, when his work often kept him in the pens both by day and by night. Whenever the Sunday cooking allowed of her absence, "Granmer" went with him, dressed for her part in a full-skirted gown, a woollen shawl and a black coal-scuttle bonnet made of puckered silk, lined with an elaborate white quilling in whose intricacies Eli took great pride. Granmer and the boy sat in the women's seats in the south aisle under the panelled gallery in which Churchwarden Stubber and his family were enthroned, and over his head Eli could hear how that dignitary shuffled his feet if the sermon exceeded half an hour. "Granfer" sat in the north aisle with the men, and by preference close to a monument of a knight and his lady. . . .

At home her (Granmer's) Prayer-book and hymn-book each lived in a holland cover, but she carried them to church wrapped in a clean white handkerchief, placing a posy of flowers on top during the greater part of the year, and sprigs of "Lad's Love," fresh or dried, to mark "the places," for Granmer was a good scholar and Granfer too, though he troubled himself but little with printed matter as a rule. (9)

Many well-to-do people were very concerned at the conditions of the poor at this time, and of those in prison. One lady sent her friend, Charles Dickens the writer, a pattern of a drab cotton material called "derry" which it was proposed to use for overalls and other purposes in the Home for Women, at Shepherd's Bush, London.

Dickens replied charmingly and sensibly:

15th November, 1856.

I return Derry. I have no doubt it's a capital article, but it's a mortal dull colour. Colour these people always want, and colour (as altered to fancy), I would always give them. . . . One colour, and that of the earth earthy, is too much with them early and late. Derry might just as well break out into a stripe, or put forth a bud, or even burst into full blown flower. Who is Derry that he is to make quakers of us all, whether we will or no! (10)

Everyday Life

(See the pictures on pp. 17–23.)

This was a time of great prosperity among the middle and upper classes in England. Servants were plentiful and the hospitality in wealthy households was famous. Here is an extract from the diary of a young American who visited England in 1875–76.

The English have carried hospitality to a fine art. . . . At breakfast the host says such and such things are going on or suggests certain plans for the visitors. What would the guests like to do? Perhaps the guests plan something between themselves, and host and hostess are free to join or not as they please. Then at lunch and afternoon tea there is a gathering of those who happen to be about, . . . It is only at dinner and in the evening that all are brought together and conversation is kept up. This makes hospitality easy and therefore frequent.

The conversation . . . was light and agreeable and such as to put a stranger perfectly at his ease. . . . Consideration and good manners here are second nature, . . . nor is there anything formal or unnatural. All retired about eleven o'clock. Breakfast is when we like in the morning.

At breakfast the servants disappeared after putting the food on the sideboard and we helped ourselves or waited on one another. The ladies seemed to expect to wait on themselves, even the Princess. . . . They start from their seats towards the side-table, but of course accept assistance from one with grace, . . . It was all so very simple and informal. (11)

The organization of a large household was a very complicated affair and the mistress had great responsibility. Here are instructions from Mrs. Beeton's Book of Household Management, *published in 1861:*

Order and Punctuality are so important to the comfort and

71

happiness of the household that every mistress should fix stated hours for meals, etc., which ought to be strictly observed by every member of the family.

ORDER OF THE HOUSEHOLD

Morning Prayers, 8.45 A.M.
"Forsake not the assembling of yourselves together."

MEALS
Breakfast (Kitchen & Nursery) . . .	8	a.m.
,, (Dining-Room)	8.30	a.m.
Kitchen Dinner.	12.30	p.m.
Luncheon	1.30	,,
Kitchen and Nursery Tea	5	,,
Dinner	6.30	,,
Kitchen Supper.	9	,,

Post Arrives   8 A.M.

"Kind words in which we feel the pressure of a hand."

Post Departs   8.30 A.M. & 6 P.M.

"A timely written letter is a rivet in the chain of affection."

Pleasures and Duties in due order linked.

Evening Prayers, 10 P.M.

The specimen card of order of the household will guide the mistress in drawing up a set of rules adapted to the special requirements of her own home. (12)

Middle-class families lived comfortably too. Here is part of a letter written by a member of an army officer's family in the 1860s:

We always had a Sunday dinner of roast beef, Yorkshire pudding, roasted potatoes, vegetables, and apple-tart in summer and plum-pudding—of a plain order—in winter, and on the side table a row of jam pots into which slices of beef and its accompaniments were put. A paper was then tied over each and they were removed to the kitchen, from whence old people or children fetched them for the refreshment of village invalids. My father—the son of a well-to-do clergyman—my mother—the daughter of a younger son of good family—had been reared in the best traditions of their day, amongst which was the duty of kindness to those less well off than themselves. (13)

Many foreigners did not think very much of the food served in taverns and restaurants in England:

I have purposely dined in twenty taverns, from the lowest to the highest, in London and elsewhere. I got large portions of fat meat and vegetables, without sauce; one is amply and wholesomely fed, but one has no pleasure in eating. In the best Liverpool eating-house they do not know how to dress a fowl. . . . their common wines, port, sherry, very hot, very spirituous, are loaded with brandy in addition; . . . our Bordeaux wines and even our Burgundies are too light for them. Amongst the middle class, ale, stout, or porter are preferred, especially brandy and water. (14)

The children of middle- and upper-class families were looked after by a children's nurse, usually called Nanny. She was responsible for them and many children only saw their parents for a short time each day. Notice how strictly they were brought up:

We children had all our meals, save our one o'clock dinner, in the nursery, and they were very plain. Porridge, bread and milk, bread fried in bacon fat, toast or bread and dripping, sometimes jam. . . . For tea, bread and butter, sometimes cake or jam, never both together. Dinner was our parents' lunch; hot or cold meat, vegetables, a pudding. Children were expected to eat what was given to them and to do as they were told. . . . One day there was Pease Pudding, to my idea, then

73

and since, a loathly compound. "Eat your portion." "Please, I can't." Threatenings of dire punishment, of the appearance of a horrid yellow mess at tea . . . at breakfast . . . nothing else until it was consumed. Obedience, and then such immediate and terrible consequences as made my parents feel that their efforts to rebuke fastidiousness had not been a success. (15)

In towns there were more and more shops where you could buy whatever you wanted. Here is part of a story which appeared in Punch *in 1858, poking fun at a young lady's shopping expedition:*

A TREMENDOUS BAG

Miss Lucy Smith went out shopping the other day, and brought home with her a tremendous bag. It was so heavy that it was as much as the page could do to bring it into the parlour to be inspected by the ladies. Upon its contents being emptied on to the dining-room table, it was found to contain: a bottle of Kiss-me-Quick, a pair of white satin shoes, a bulky packet of gloves (cleaned), a dozen rolls of cotton, a paper of pearl buttons (to mend Papa's shirts), a box of cough lozenges, a bundle of violet powder, a kettle-holder, ten yards of blue ribbon, a pack of club cards, . . . a pot of bear's grease, a pound of jujubes, a velvet necktie, three cambric handkerchiefs with "Lucy" embroidered in gay flowers in the corner, a pair of mittens, a small tin can supposed to contain acidulated drops, beads and long pins and gold daggers and imitation coins for the hair, fifteen yards of best longcloth, a bundle of brushes and small jars of gum for potichomanie work, small curling irons, several small pots containing perfumes, . . . numerous papers of different varieties of Berlin wool, . . . two ounces of shot to sew round the bottom of one's dress, seven yards of edging for night-caps, a set of doll's tea things, two packages of bird-seed for the canary, a bath bun, . . . Miss Smith was not a little pleased with the results of her day's sport, having brought down every one of the articles . . . in the space of little more than four hours and a quarter. (16)

Most girls expected to marry when they grew up, and to have a

74

family, but opportunities of other work were increasing. A writer, in 1887, pointed out how things had changed in fifty years:

The fifty years of the Queen's reign have brought about an immense alteration in the position of women. They are not, indeed, admitted to the Parliamentary suffrage, in spite of strenuous efforts, . . . but they can vote in other than Parliamentary elections, . . . The real change, however, has been a social change. Women are now permitted to qualify in medicine; in one university at least the degrees that are open to men are open to them; in almost every other University they are admitted to examination, and in some they have residential colleges organized on exactly the same basis as the colleges for male students. Still more important are the changes that have been made by law in the relation of wives towards husbands and children, and of women and children to their employers. The tendency of modern legislation has been to advance wives from a position where they had scarcely any rights at all to a position of almost complete equality with their husbands. (17)

But there were great contrasts in the ways in which people lived and in many parts of England poor families were in great misery. Here is a description of ". . . the conditions of the wage-earning class in York" towards the end of the century:

Spinster. Blind. Two rooms. Earns a little by knitting. Parish relief; also 2s. per week from a former employer. Very clean. Spends a lot of time with relatives. This house shares one water-tap with seven other houses, and one closet with one other. Rent 2s. 6d.

The food consisted largely of a dreary succession of bread, dripping, and tea; bacon, bread and coffee, with only a little butcher's meat, and none of the extras and but little of the variety which serves to make meals interesting and appetizing. . . .

The clothing is often as inadequate as the food; this is notably the case amongst the uncomplaining poor, who receive few gifts of clothing, their clean and tidy appearance not suggesting that although the exterior garments are tidy, the under-garments are totally inadequate to keep out the cold.

"If there's anything extra to buy, such as a pair of boots for one of the children," a woman told one of my investigators, "me and the children goes without dinner—or mebbe only 'as a cup o' tea and a bit o' bread, but Jim (her husband) ollers takes 'is dinner to work, and I giv it 'im as usual. 'E never knows we go without, and I never tells 'im." (18)

An important Churchman, Canon Barnett, described dreadful conditions in letters to his friends:

The death-rate among the children of the poor is double that among the children of the rich. . . . The occupants of the prisons are mostly of one class—the poor. . . . It is because they have not the means to hide their vices under respectable forms that the poor go to prison and not the rich.

Too long have the poor been forgotten by the rich, . . . The ordinary condition of families who are forced to live in one room, to pay their way, find their pleasure, and prepare for disease or old age on 18s. a week ought to be known.

Dock labourers, who . . . cannot hope to get four days a week at 3s. a day, tailoresses who cannot get more than 3d. for a boy's suit if it is to be sold for 4s. 10d.; these, and many like them, endure evils not to be described in words. (19)

Skilled workers, on the other hand, were living fairly comfortably:

The houses generally have a frontage of from 15 to 17 feet, and usually contain five rooms and a scullery. . . . The sitting-room often contains a piano and an overmantel in addition to the usual furniture, not to speak of ornamental mantelpieces of imitation marble and brightly-tiled hearths. It is chiefly used on Sundays, or as a receiving-room for visitors who are not on terms sufficiently intimate to be asked into the kitchen. Occasionally it is used by the husband when he has writing to do in connection with friendly or other societies, or by the children when practising music. The real living-room is the kitchen, rendered cheerful and homely by the large open grate and the good oven, unknown in the south, but familiar in the north of England where coal is cheap, and where the thrifty housewife bakes her own bread. The floor of this room is commonly covered with linoleum, although a large home-made hearthrug may lend an air of solid comfort. A sofa, albeit of horse-hair or American cloth, an arm-chair, polished tins, and china ornaments on the high mantelpiece, add the subtle touch of homeliness. Though small, the scullery, which is provided with a sink, water-tap, and "copper" for washing, contributes to the comfort of the house. . . . Few working men's houses in York are fitted with a bath. (20)

A writer at the end of the century compared the lives of farm workers with those of others living eighty or ninety years before:

Were the country folk in our English villages at the beginning of this (*nineteenth*) century more or less content with their lot than they are today? Were they happier or the reverse? . . .

The agricultural labourers of today are certainly better clad, more luxuriously fed, have far more leisure, are better educated, and are rapidly becoming better housed than their forefathers a century ago. And if these are the main constituents of happiness, than they are happier. . . .

Perhaps the saddest characteristic of the men of the present, as compared with the men of the past, is that the men of the past were certainly more self-dependent, more resourceful, more kindly, courteous and contented with their lot than their descendants are. (21)

Position and money were still thought to entitle people to special favours, as this little story shows:

He (Lord Coleridge) told me that at one time he went with the Duke of Wellington to a railway station, and on coming to the booking office found there was some delay about the tickets, the men asking those in line to wait. Then Coleridge said, "I see, Your Grace, that they make us wait like the rest." As soon as the ticket-seller heard that there was a duke in line, he immediately stopped what he was doing and insisted upon giving them their tickets ahead of the rest. (22)

English people have for a long time been very fond of processions and pageants. The Diamond Jubilee of Queen Victoria's Coronation in

1887 was a very special occasion. Here is how a choir boy at Windsor described the day in his diary:

On the twenty-second of June, Tuesday, we got up very early, and started from Windsor at 5.45 a.m., arriving in London about seven o'clock. Then we went from Waterloo to St. Paul's Cathedral. Then while we were waiting to get in, we sat on a stone near the railings and watched the men walking about in their robes and uniforms.

Then we got on to the lawn round St. Paul's, and we went and got our food, which we had left there the day before when we went to the rehearsal.

Then we went down into St. Paul's Crypt and we ate a few sandwiches; then we went up and had some lemon squash mixed with water from a tap (I remember how we wondered if the water was all right, as it seemed to spring up from the graves in the churchyard).

Then, after looking round the Cathedral, which was very jolly, we descended to the Crypt again and put on our surplices. Then up again and sat in the nave watching the Bishops and Archbishops of all countries, and the Gentlemen of the Queen's Bodyguard, carrying their axes studded all over with jewels.

One of them gave me his to hold, and went away for some time, and I began to wonder what I could do with it if he didn't come back. It would have looked very funny for a choir-boy to carry such a weapon. He happened to come back just as we were ordered to go out into our places on the steps, and I was asking Mr. Kempton, one of our basses, what on earth I should do with it. So he was only just in time.

Oh, it was a sight that we saw. The roads were all lined with Jack tars and soldiers. All the British troops were there, I should think. There were besides lots of soldiers of all regiments to play the band. . . .

Now I must tell you of some things that struck me about it all. The Queen was dressed in black silk with silver on it. She had a black bonnet made of lace, trimmed with white flowers and with an aigrette of diamonds. She carried a white lace sunshade, and she had a fan. Her parasol was up. Her horses

78

looked exactly like a circus. Lord Roberts looked very well on his famous Arabian steed.

All the princes looked very well on their chargers. The Queen looked very well indeed and ever so happy. Everybody looked very well. On the other hand, lots of people fainted in the crowds.

The Te Deum was most exciting, and made a grand noise with all the bands and the great choir. Sir George Martin conducted, and all the people joined in the singing of the Old Hundredth and "God Save the Queen." After the National Anthem the Archbishop of Canterbury called out, "Three Cheers for the Queen." . . .

After all this the Procession moved away and left us in peace to eat our dinner on the lawn in front of St. Paul's. It seemed funny to eat in a churchyard, but we were hungry all the same, and the graves didn't spoil our appetites one bit. (23)

Education

(See the pictures on pp. 24–26.)

Until 1870 there was no law compelling children to attend school. Many children of well-to-do parents were taught at home by a tutor or a governess. Others went to private schools and the boys, when they were 14, were sent to one of the many public schools which were founded during this period. There were also grammar schools, most of which charged high fees, and some boarding schools for girls.

Poorer children, if they went to school at all, went to charity schools which had been founded by the various churches. Here is a letter, written in 1868, which tells us of the conditions:

The masters and mistresses of ragged schools declare that the children continually cry with hunger, and frequently fall exhausted from their seats for want of food, and that it is impossible to teach them in such a state. (24)

Many people were concerned about the situation and wanted to alter the law so that working hours were shorter and all children had some schooling. In 1860 an attempt was made to bring a Bill about this into the House of Commons. Notice what the objections were:

There was a Bill for making it compulsory on the employers of the labour of children under twelve years old, to have a certificate that the child was learning to read and write, and had twenty hours of teaching per month—nothing like an hour a day. But so monstrous an Innovation frightened the House. Mr. Henley . . . said that people were not to eat unless they worked, but were not commanded to read and write; Mr. Buxton . . . said there were thousands of children too idle, wicked or stupid to learn, . . . Mr. Hardy . . . said that the children of the poor were taught quite enough to enable them to do the duties they were intended for; . . . the Bill was thrown out. (25)

Some of the private schools were good, but most were very bad. In 1861 a Government committee reported that it had received:

"distressing evidence as to the character of most of the private schools, which were usually the only ones to be found in the districts whose need was attracting special attention. These were often taught by discharged servants or barmaids, outdoor paupers, small traders, washerwomen, cripples, drunkards, consumptive and very aged persons—those, in short, who had no more profitable resource than such a school afforded. Many of the schools were held in lofts, bedrooms, cellars, kitchens, shops, workshops, or other available but unsuitable places; where the children, generally little more than infants, tumbled over one another 'like puppies in a kennel.' Attendance, always irregular, ceased altogether at an early age, and the pupils, who had learnt next to nothing, forgot even this within the next twelve months." (26)

Lord Shaftesbury, a great social reformer, gradually led public opinion to realize that the Government must provide better education for all children and that attendance must be made compulsory.

The Education Act of 1870 provided for elementary education for all children in England and Wales, and School Boards were elected to carry out the Act. So the schools built were called "Board Schools." Attendance was compulsory, but until 1891 parents had to pay a small fee for sending their children.

Here are some of the things that the 1870 Education Act laid down.

. . . there shall be provided for every school district . . . accommodation in public elementary schools . . . for all the children resident in such district for whose elementary education efficient and suitable provision is not otherwise made . . .

. . . it shall not be required, as a condition of any child being admitted into the school, that he shall attend or abstain from attending any Sunday-school, or any place of religious worship, . . .

. . . the school shall be open at all times to the inspection of any of Her Majesty's inspectors. . . .

Every child attending a school provided by any school board shall pay a weekly fee, but the school board may . . . remit the whole or any part of such fee . . . when they are of opinion that the parent . . . is unable to pay the same.

. . . if, on the ground of poverty of the inhabitants of any place, . . . it is expedient for the interests of education to provide a school at which no fees shall be required from the scholars, the school board may provide such a school.

Every school board may . . . make bye-laws for . . . the following purposes

1. Requiring the parents of children . . . of not less than 5 years nor more than 13 years . . . to cause such children (unless there is some reasonable excuse) to attend school.
2. Determining the time during which children are so to attend school. . . .

. . . . any bye-law . . . requiring a child between 10 and 13 years of age to attend school shall provide for the total or partial exemption of such child from the obligation to attend school if one of Her Majesty's inspectors certifies that such child has reached a (specified) standard of education.

. . . no penalty imposed for the breach of any bye-law shall exceed . . . five shillings for each offence. (27)

Here are entries in the school log-book of Miss Annie Pink, a teacher in a village school, soon after the Education Act had been passed: Evidently Miss Pink was a good teacher and the children very much enjoyed her school:

Feb. 1, 1872   School Fees. Labourers' children 2d. a week. Second class farmers and tradesmen 3s. 6d. a quarter. First class farmers 5s. a quarter.

April 26, 1886   Easter Monday. 38 of the children having given up the Good Friday tea drinking, they joined us in a most enjoyable half holiday. We commenced play at 2 p.m. by scrambling for nuts and ginger-bread, then played games until 4 p.m. when children assembled in the school house for tea—comprising tea and coffee, cakes, buns, twists, pork pies, sausage rolls, tarts, cheese cakes, bread and butter, eggs and jam. Games were then resumed till 8 p.m. when they all assembled again for supper, the same as tea, ginger beer taking the place of coffee and tea. All was much enjoyed and the children dispersed most merrily.

March 1, 1886 Have had, for the last fortnight, very snowy and almost impassable roads; have had a considerable number of the children in the school house to work sums in the dinner hour. So many begged to attend that I have kept quite a little merry private school much to the childrens' pleasure, for after they have worked 8 sums correctly, if time allows I give them a little fireside amusement.

March 15, 1883 I kept the whole school in for three-quarters of an hour after the proper time for dismissal, until a boy had publicly shewn submission and sorrow for disobedience.

Feb. 16, 1884 One of the elder boys behaved very badly in the school this afternoon, and threw a cane with which I was going to punish him across the room. I at once made him leave school determined not to allow him to re-enter without a full and public apology.

June 5, 1886 A great disturbance took place in the school from the visit of a policeman to search for a missing hat which had been with several more mischieviously hidden by a very naughty little boy. The policeman handcuffed the culprit and another boy (innocent) to frighten the rest of the school to whom he held out several threats. (28)

"Board" schools were inspected every year. The visit of an Inspector was an important event because the amount of money that the Board of

Education allowed a school to spend during the next year depended on whether the Inspector was satisfied with what he found on his visit.

Teachers were paid "by results." The Inspector questioned the class and if enough children could answer well, the teacher might get an increase in salary. In this extract from The School Manager's Series of Reading Books adapted to the requirements of the New Code, *the teacher (Mary) is anxious about the visit of the Inspector, but Sophy does not mind at all.*

For Standard 4. (A dialogue between Mary Saunders, a pupil teacher, and the rebellious Sophy Williams, aged 12.)

Mary   You must look sharp, Sophy, or you will not have made up your attendances before the Inspector comes. What has kept you away so much from school?

Sophy   I don't know—one thing and another—sometimes mother wanted me, sometimes my shoes were bad, and my sister has been at home from service, and I wanted to be along of her. . . . Never you be afraid. It's only the three r's that the Spectre comes to see about isn't it?

Mary   I do wish you would learn to pronounce your words properly. "in-spect-or" means one who looks *into* a thing. "Spectre" means a ghost.

Sophy   And the best name of the two, for the thoughts of his coming seem to frighten everybody like a ghost—but I am not a bit afraid. I can read and write and sum and that's all that's expected.

Mary   But if you read so that nobody understands you, if you write such a bad hand that nobody can read it, and if your sums are always wrong; what's the use?

(29)

This "School for Poor Law Children" at Forest Gate, near London, was very different from Miss Pink's Village School. One of the Managers described how it had improved, however, between 1875 and 1885:

The children were dressed in a uniform, and no one had his or her own clothes. They wore any that happened to fit, as

they were handed out on the day of the weekly change. . . .
Silence reigned at meal times. The regulation weight of food
was handed out to each child according to its age, but regard-
less of its size, appetite, taste or physical condition. Dull food
dully eaten does not conduce to robust health.

The hours out of school were not play hours. The girls
scrubbed the vast areas . . . of boarded rooms, but they were
not allowed even to do it together. Each child was placed a
few yards off the other. The boys quarrelled or shivered in the
yards, unless they enjoyed bullying a smaller "chap" . . .

The children were not called by their names. Each was
commonly addressed as "child." They had no toys, no library,
no Sunday school, no places in which to keep personal possessions, no playing-fields, no night garments, no prizes, no
flowers, no pets, no pictures on the walls, no pleasures in
music, no opportunities for seeing the world outside the school
walls. . . .

Ten years later . . . the children romped in playing-fields,
dug and delved in little gardens, talked busily at meals, wore
night garments, owned three sets of day apparel; possessed
toys, large ones, in common; small treasures, such as dolls,
puzzle books and boxes, which now lived in personally owned
"lockers" . . .

Bare rooms had been decorated with pictures, and high
hope was to be read through many a motto on colour-washed
walls. Flowers grew in the windows, cats kittened in the
laundry, canaries sang . . . Concerts were given almost
weekly . . . Each girl was called by her Christian prefix. Each
boy by his sire's name. . . . (30)

*Another writer compared the Public Schools of 1887 with the same
schools fifty years earlier:*

The Queen's accession found a great man (Dr. Arnold) at
work at Rugby. . . . In his day the schools were few, their tone
generally not healthy. . . . Even now (1887) our system of
public school education is open to criticism and debate . . . but,
as a rule, in any of the multitude of first-grade schools to be
found throughout the country, well-trained and sympathetic

masters make it their business to interest their boys, and to a great extent they succeed . . . we have now not one Rugby, but a score; and, just below them, a hundred schools to which a parent may send his son in the certainty that he will not be grossly neglected. (31)

One of the reasons why so much of education was so poor, was that it was thought that anybody could teach children. Here are two advertisements which appeared in Punch *in the 1860s:*

Grammar School, W———— R————. Wanted immediately, a Second Assistant Master, to teach thoroughly writing and arithmetic, also junior English subjects. Must be a good cricketer and round-arm bowler. Character to bear strictest investigation. Salary £40, increasing to £60. (32)

A Single Lady, aged 36, with a limited income, offers £20 per annum and two hours' daily instruction to one or two Children in English and the rudiments of music and French, in return for her Board. (33)

But the idea was growing that those who were going to teach should be trained for the job. Here is a letter written in the 1850's describing "An Institution called Whitelands":

The system of training there seems to me perfect and they make a very great point of needlework, particularly cutting out, and shirt-making and gown-making as well as fine work. There seems such a desire to make them really humble unpretending Village Teachers, making them clean and cook and iron (not wash) that they mayn't fancy themselves fine ladies *because* they teach them Geography & History and so on. The only things they don't set them to are scouring and washing, and they say "The nature of these employments (scouring and washing) is such as to unfit the hands for fine needlework in which it is absolutely essential the mistresses should excel. But every effort is made to give them just views of the worth of humble domestic duties on the performance of which so much of the comfort of both rich and poor depend— a happy change may be hoped for in the race of young servants who issue from our schools if we obtain mistresses able and willing to instruct them in the proper method of performing the simpler offices of their station. . . ." I have copied this bit out, I think it sounds so sensible. (34)

In 1886 The Education Reform League issued a report, setting out its aims:

The object of the Education Reform League is to enlist the co-operation of the working classes in the effort to infuse more life into the dry bones of State-aided Elementary Education. Its aims include:

1. University education for teachers in primary schools.
2. Equal opportunities for all children to attain their highest capability by continuity of training—technical, physical, and intellectual.
3. Improvements in the system of inspection.
4. The more general employment of school buildings and playgrounds for the people's benefit. (35)

In 1899 an advertisement appeared in The Labour Annual, *announcing a very important development:*

Ruskin Hall, Oxford, is remarkable as being the first and only real Labour College in the world. Board, lodging and all living expenses are to be only 10s. weekly, or £25 per year. Tuition and tutor's fees are 10s. monthly in addition. The College makes no attempt to train barristers, clergymen, financiers or military officers, but it endeavours to furnish the most complete training in the world for such members of the rising democracy as may desire to possess that knowledge which, . . . is power. Situated in Oxford, all students will share in the incomparable advantages of one of the world's greatest Universities. It will be the only college in the world sufficiently modern to base its teaching on the complete transformation of industry and commerce, and all the conditions and environment of life by the progress of modern science, invention and discovery. It will deal sympathetically yet practically with absolutely new and unprecedented conditions of existence, to which man has yet to learn to adjust his relations. The principal object of Ruskin Hall is to train political and educational leaders from among the ranks of the common people: leaders

87

capable of directing that widespread and irresistible movement which, if progress is to continue, must sooner or later wrest civilization from the clutch of obsolete custom and organized self-interest or greed, substitute therefor juster and humaner conditions, and thus help to coordinate social institutions with the larger requirements of the race. Prospectus and further particulars may be obtained from C. A. Beard, correspondent, 41, Banbury-rd., Oxford. (36)

Women had been agitating for some time that the education of girls should be as good as the education of boys. But many people feared that if women became better educated they would be less feminine and less able to be good wives and mothers. Here are some satirical verses which appeared in Punch *in 1884:*

The Woman of the Future! She'll be deeply read, that's certain,
With all the education gained at Newnham or at Girton;
She'll puzzle men in Algebra with horrible quadratics,
Dynamics, and the mysteries of higher mathematics;
Or, if she turns to classic tomes a literary roamer,
She'll give you bits of Horace or sonorous lines from Homer.

You take a maiden in to dine, and find, with consternation,
She scorns the light frivolities of modern conversation;
And not for her the latest bits of fashionable chatter,
Her pretty head is wellnigh full of more important matter;
You talk of Drama or Burlesque, theatric themes pursuing,
She only thinks of what the Dons at Oxford may be doing.

The Woman of the Future may be very learned-looking,
But dare we ask if she'll know aught of housekeeping or cooking?
She'll read far more, and that is well, than empty-headed
    beauties,
But has she studied with it all a woman's chiefest duties?
We wot she'll ne'er acknowledge, till her heated brain grows
    cooler,
That Woman, not the Irishman, should be the true home-ruler.

(37)

Leisure

(See the pictures on pp. 27–31.)

Servants were plentiful, so well-to-do families had far more leisure than anyone has nowadays. But those working in the factories, in shops and on the farms had hardly any leisure at all. Hours were very long and Sunday was the only free day in the week. It was on the whole a dreary day in England and many of the poorer people, whose homes were wretched, spent a good deal of their Sundays in the public houses. In 1854 this was referred to in the report of a committee which was enquiring into the running of public houses.

Your Committee cannot conclude this portion of their report without calling attention to the fact of how few places of rational enjoyment are open to the great mass of the population on Sunday which serve as a counter attraction to the public house.

Sir Joseph Paxton states that "from three to five and even so many as 800 persons used to come on Sundays from Sheffield to go over the house and gardens at Chatsworth. They had to go afterwards to the public houses for their vehicles but used never to sit sotting and drinking nor to cause disturbances. About ten years since, his Grace the Duke of Devonshire in answer to a petition from his servants (who found the duty of attendance both on weekdays and Sundays too onerous) closed Chatsworth altogether on the Sunday. Nearly the same number of persons as before came into the neighbourhood on Sundays, but having no longer the interest of viewing the park and the house, they used to revel at the public houses and create disturbance. On representation of these facts the Duke reopened, not the house, but the park and all the outer grounds. Since then there has been no difficulty about the public house nuisance." . . . (38)

By the later part of the period, Sunday had become rather less dreary. Here is a newspaper report of a speech by the President of the Sunday Society in 1895:

. . . the advocates of the Sunday opening of museums, picture-galleries, and libraries have now no serious opponents. . . . The question now is what is to be done with the victory? On the one side, the opening of museums, picture-galleries, gardens and libraries is not sufficient if it is not made lawful to use public halls for music and lectures. On the other side, Sunday must be protected from the demon of greed, which would fill its hours with the noise of strife and strain, substitute for the week-day competition of work a Sunday competition of pleasure, and drive from life the feeling of quiet. (39)

Musical evenings were popular in middle-class homes:

The Musical Evening was a free-and-easy affair. . . . People . . . brought their music with them in a little music-case, mostly of patent leather. This they left in the hall with their hats and coats, or in the bedroom with their wraps, according to their sex. They seldom took it straight into the drawing-room with them. It was not good form to show that they were eager to perform, though it was the deadliest insult if their hostess forgot to ask them; they never went there again. (40)

There was no radio, no television, no cinema, so people expected to amuse themselves. Girls had to be what was called "accomplished":

Whether they had any aptitude or not, they had "accomplishments" thrust upon them. The most general was music—as exemplified by piano-playing. The girl of those times had a music-mistress, and the family endured with resignation the ceaseless hours of note-fumbling which ensued before even a simple tune stumblingly emerged. The practising was even worse. But, then, it was expected of every girl. She simply had to be able to play the piano. (41)

Pantomimes were favourite family entertainments at Christmas time, and circuses also. Here is a description written in 1867 of a circus which opened at the New Holborn Amphitheate in that year:

Up in the gallery we are not a dignified audience, and we enjoy ourselves immensely. We laugh till the tears run down our faces, and stamp and kick our admiration as if we wanted to kick the boards in (and pay a precipitate visit to the chignons in the balcony). A good many of us are children, and throw ourselves back in our seats and actually scream with delight. Who shall sing the praises of the clown? How clever he is to be sure! How madly he dashes his flannel fool's cap on to the carpet, and with what gusto he runs amongst the attendants, tumbles friend and foe head over heels, tears up the paper discs, and stuffs the fragments into his pocket for a handkerchief. How thorough is his enjoyment of mischief; and how impossible it seems for him to keep quiet for a moment. Then, what side-splitting jokes he makes. . . . (42)

During the 1860s the music halls were patronized mainly by working-class people. Many in the audience were very poor and dissatisfied with general conditions, and their discontent was sometimes expressed in the songs the performers sang. Here is an example:

THE DAILY NEWS

As thro' this precious world you steer,
    This bit of counsel take from me;
Don't you believe all that you hear,
    And only half of what you see,
The *Standard*, *Star* and *Telegraph*,
    Of what's going on give their own views;
But at their information laugh—
    I'll tell you what's the daily news.
        Chorus.
The newspapers are all my eye,
    So don't the *Times* or *Sun* peruse;
Just listen to me, and I'll try
    To tell you what's the daily news.
The daily news is this, my boys—
    The rich get richer every day,
Monopolizing all life's joys,
    While the poor the piper have to pay.

91

French cooks and tailors for the great,
　　For the small hard fare, and oft no shoes;
And hundreds forced to emigrate—
　　That's *bona-fide* daily news.　　　　　　(43)

*Many people who had not been to school were anxious to learn to
read and write. There was a widespread thirst for knowledge and in
1887 one writer commented:*

. . . at the present time the humblest household has at its
command not only the news of the day, seasoned and illustrated with plenty of political discussion, but, on the one side,
a multitude of cheap periodicals to provide amusement and
social and technical instruction, and, on the other, the master-
pieces of the literature of the past. For a penny a week the
working carpenter or engineer can inform himself of the
latest improvements that science has introduced into his craft;
the country boy can learn in a clear and accurate form what is
known of the birds and butterflies of his neighbourhood. For
ninepence a man can buy the whole of Shakespeare, and
"National Libraries" and "World Libraries" provide him with
chosen portions of Milton and Addison, of Bacon and Pope,
at threepence a volume. (44)

*Other forms of amusement, too, were increasingly available to
poorer people. Working hours were very long, compared with present-
day standards, but in 1887 a social worker wrote:*

Every class amuses itself more; or rather, amusements which
were formerly thought to be the birthright of the upper classes
alone are now shared by the many. Prize-fighting, dog-fighting
and cock-fighting have been condemned, first by public
opinion and then by law, and their places have been taken by
sports and pastimes which may often indeed be wanting in
refinement, but which are at least relatively free from brutality.
. . . The amusement that interests all classes most is still horse-
racing, and horse-racing . . . does harm as well as good; but
cricket, football and other athletic sports have simultaneously
developed and annually arouse an increasing interest in the
minds of the people. (45)

The Boat Race between Oxford and Cambridge was popular with people of all kinds. Can you notice any differences between the race nowadays and this one in 1868:

There is no scene so thoroughly English as that which the banks of the Thames present on the morning of the University Boat Race. The excited, eager crowds which line the whole distance of the course, the eccentric fleet of steamboats, which seemingly defy all order and regulation, and the crowd of horsemen, good, bad and indifferent, who endeavour to fight their way along the towpath; there is no other country that can boast of such sights as these; for, be it remembered, this is no pleasant picnic under a summer sky, such as to the many constitutes their whole pleasure in the uproarious Derby fair on Epsom Downs, or on the more decorous and fashionable gala days of Ascot and Goodwood. The pitiless east wind may ruffle the bosom of our mighty father of waters, yet not the less does the fairest bevy of beauty in the world brave its cold kiss. (46)

Cricket was the most popular pastime of men of all classes. A writer in 1864 explained some of the reasons for the popularity:

Prince, peer, parson, peeler and peasant all participate in the game. It is professionally taught in schools. . . . The clergy award it their support; nearly every shire in England has its county club. Heads of large mercantile firms shrewdly encourage cricket among their employees; factories turn out their elevens. The government patronize the game among their hard-working civil service men; and among the thews and sinnews of most large towns the Saturday afternoon during the season is now termed "the cricket afternoon." (47)

The Australians won the Test Match for the first time in 1882, by only seven runs. Next morning the following appeared in The Sporting Times:

In affectionate remembrance of English Cricket, which died at the Oval on the 29th of August, 1882. Deeply lamented by a large circle of sorrowing friends and acquaintances. R.I.P. (N.B. The body will be cremated and the ashes taken to Australia.) (48)

The following year the successful eleven returned from Australia

93

with a small earthenware urn containing a heap of ashes that had been presented with all solemnity by the women of Melbourne!

Not many people could afford to go away for holidays, but the development of railways was beginning to make it possible for more families to travel. Here is part of a rather pompous article in a journal of 1871:

The holiday excursions of the olden time were restricted to a small number of places, at short distances from home, and were indulged in by a limited number of persons. Now, however, abundant facilities are provided by our railway companies for excursions, which, from the metropolis, take all directions, and include a large number of very attractive places of resort. . . . To the great mass of the people, improved means of locomotion afford opportunities not enjoyed by the last generation for physical and intellectual relaxation, and, we dare to say, moral development and amelioration. The time has been, even in the life of the present generation, that the great mass of countrymen knew nothing of "town," and Londoners knew nothing of country. Places twenty miles distant, and the occupations and habits of the people dwelling there, were as much *terra incognita* as Chinese Tartary and its inhabitants. The railways and holiday excursion trains . . . have been the means of enlarging and correcting the conceptions concerning men, manners and places of millions of persons . . . dispelling such grotesque crudities as that Scotland is a town, and Lancashire a village, the inhabitants of which are personally known to one another. (49)

But in her diary Mary Gladstone described a visit to the seaside which was evidently not at all pompous:

Fri. Aug. 11 (1871) . . . At 3 off in 2 open carriages to the sea shore for a picnic, 7 miles off . . . sang glees the whole way, great fun. The meal a triumphant success, specially the fire, and afterwards building a sand castle at which we all worked like ants, and made the "Sea look a fool." It was amusing to see the gravity and earnestness of them all over the designing of it, and their arguments about the fortifications. Stopped till 9.30 and drove home in the dark. (50)

The Arts

The new, rich, middle-class industrialists did not have the taste of the aristocrats and the country gentry who had been patrons of the arts in the eighteenth century. Painters were affected by a sentimental interest in past styles and usually tried to "tell a story" in their pictures.

In 1850, after visiting all the exhibitions open in London, Punch asked:

Is painting a living art in England at this moment?

Is there a nineteenth century?

Are there men and women round about us, doing, acting, suffering?

Is the subject-matter of Art, clothes? Or is it men and women, their actions, passions and sufferings?

If Art is vital, should it not somehow find food among living events, interests, and incidents? Is our life, at this day, so unideal, so devoid of all sensuous and outward picturesqueness and beauty, that for subjects to paint we must needs go back to . . . Charles the Second, or William the Third, or George the Second? (51)

But most people had no doubts about the modern, photographic style of painting, and flocked to the opening of the Grosvenor Gallery on May 1, 1877:

The fine new Art-Gallery in Bond Street, provided by the liberality and enterprise of Sir Coutts Lindsay, has this week been opened for the first public exhibition of pictures and sculpture. . . . (52)

All the world was—bewilderingly—there . . . I remember being impressed by their long hair, and bushy faces, and short jackets—for many were not in morning clothes. There was one enormous picture . . . in the foreground a gigantic cabbage with other specimens of agriculture next it, and a great crowd blocked it up and talked about the "realism of the cabbage!" (53)

Here is a description of the pictures and decoration in the home of one of Charles Darwin's family in the 1880s:

The house was full of lovely things; Aunt Ellen's own taste in art had more of the vogue of the moment. There was just a trace of greenery-yallery and Japanese fans about her own rooms; and the nursery was rather pitch-piney and bleak. In the drawing-room hung a large engraving after a painting by Fred Walker, "The Harvest Moon," in which a rustic character with a scythe and several maidens wended their classical way across the face of the full moon. You could almost date the marriage from that picture alone, it was so often given as a wedding present about 1883. I knew two other of the best academic houses in Cambridge where it was the chief adornment of the drawing-room. There was a small cast of the "Venus of Milo," and all about the house there hung large photographs of the Best Pictures. . . . Even in those cultivated circles the French Impressionists had not yet been heard of, though J. F. Millet had got through. (54)

Ballad concerts were popular and were held regularly at the Queen's Hall, in London:

At these concerts there might be one or two instrumental items, but the staple fare was ballads and lots of them. They were well sung by the most eminent of vocalists and the reception at these concerts of the songs themselves showed the publishers whether they had launched a success or not. (55)

If a woman did not marry there was little she could do except live with her parents, or work as a governess or a servant. But writing was now accepted as a "genteel" thing to do and there were a number of women novelists. Mary Gladstone wrote in her diary:

Hawarden, Jan. 1, 1881. I have never mentioned the overwhelming loss to the world in the death of George Eliot. There have been some fine words about it in the papers, but none approaching to those of Lord Acton. "In problems of life and thought which baffled Shakespeare disgracefully, her touch was unfailing. No writer ever lived who had anything like her power of manifold but disinterested and impartially observant sympathy. If Sophocles or Cervantes had lived in the light of our culture, ... George Eliot might have had a rival." ... (56)

The two great stars of the theatrical world were Ellen Terry and Henry Irving. Mary Gladstone was a great play-goer and wrote in her diary:

(a) London, Monday, July 8 (1878) To *Olivia*. Oh, how I enjoyed it. Ellen Terry is beautiful in it and pathetic beyond words. The story is lofty in tone and well put together from the *Vicar of Wakefield*, some of the wording lovely, all the parts well done and some quite admirable, scenery, dresses, etc., perfect, everybody cries, and we watched Miss Kate Vaughan weeping with great interest.

(b) London, Tues. 25 Feb. (1879) Again to Lyceum. This time Ophelia carried me more off my feet and I could not take my eyes off her. It's awful the pathos of it—her voice, countenance, attitudes, gestures, etc., perfect. He (Irving), too, is almost inspired in the great scene with her, the struggles between his bitterness and love, the cruel taunting words, ... the conflicting feelings that fly across his face. The whole scene keeps one breathless. ... (57)

Travel and Communications

(See the pictures on pp. 32–38.)

The first excitement of travelling by train was over and people were beginning to find fault with the services that were available. Even the second-class carriages were so badly lighted that passengers took candle reading-lamps with them. Candles for these could be bought at Smith's bookstalls. There were no restaurant cars until 1882, so until then everybody carried their own food. There were no corridors, so even after 1882 those who wanted a meal had to transfer into the restaurant car when the train stopped.

Here is a Frenchman's view of English trains in the eighteen-fifties:

It is a great mistake to believe in the speed and excellent management of the British railways, which are under the free control of companies who can treat travellers exactly as they please. Although the fares are very high they take advantage of any event likely to attract the public to raise their prices. They even take off the third-class carriages and sometimes the seconds also, so as to oblige one to travel first. The cheapest seats are mostly uncovered, and in a country where it rains perpetually can one imagine anything more barbarous? The second-class compartments have wooden benches and back rests, no upholstering of any kind. The windows are unglazed and only provided with wooden shutters. These carriages are so dirty that it is difficult to believe they are ever swept. They do not have special goods trains, but load everything on to the passenger trains, hence the interminable delays. They have also a most trying habit of collecting tickets in the train itself just before it reaches its destination. I remember one Sunday, outside Brighton, three collectors taking the tickets of 2,000 passengers waiting unprotected in the broiling sun between a rock and a brick wall. (58)

In 1863 the engine driver and fireman of a luggage train were fined 15s. each at Oxford for being found drunk and incapable on their engine:

They declared in the presence of the Company's Officers and without contradiction, that their day was fourteen hours, and that owing to extra pressure, they had only had seventeen hours sleep the whole of the week. . . . On whom should fall the blame and punishment? On the men, outworn, and driven to stimulants as a substitute for sleep or a support under exhaustion, or on the managers of the Company, who thus overwork, or, in other words, underpay their servants? (59)

A great many parts of the country were still not served by any railway and people still travelled by road. Here is an account of an adventurous coach journey in 1857:

I left Dunrobin after breakfast on Saturday morning . . . and arrived in London on Monday . . . at 11 a.m. . . . We got into the mail at Golspie and took our places to Inverness. At Tain, the first stage, we walked on, leaving the coach to overtake us. After walking three miles, and no coach coming, we got alarmed, and on enquiry of the first man we fell in with, found we had come the wrong way, and that the mail had gone on. We started on our return to Tain, and falling in with a good Samaritan in the shape of a banker in that place, he took us up in his gig, and drove us back to the inn, where we took post, and followed the mail to Inverness, where we arrived an hour after it. There we slept, and at five minutes before five on Sunday morning we were in the coach again, and arrived at Perth at six o'clock, making 117 miles in thirteen hours. In twenty minutes more we were in the mail train, and reached Euston Square safe and sound at eleven o'clock, doing the distance between Perth and London in seventeen and a half hours. (60)

Bicycling was the new craze towards the end of the century. Here is the advertisement of a ladies' cycling school in 1895:

The Royal Cycle Repository and Riding School is the Best and Largest School in London for Ladies or Gentlemen to learn Cycle Riding. Terms till proficient 10/6. Bicycles or tricycles bought for cash in any condition, or taken in exchange for new ones. Utmost value allowed. Auction Sales every Wednesday, at 1 prompt. Private Sales and Exchanges, and Riding Taught Daily. Hours, 8 till 9. Machines Let on Hire by the day, week or month with option of purchase. Open 8 a.m. to 9 p.m.

81, Euston Road, King's Cross, London (facing the Midland Grand Hotel). (61)

People of all kinds enjoyed the new means of getting about:

The Bicycling craze came in when we were just about at the right age to enjoy it. At first even "safety" bicycles were too dangerous and improper for ladies to ride, and they had to have tricycles. My mother had (I believe) the first female tricycle in Cambridge; and I had a little one, and we used to go out for family rides, all together; my father in front on a bicycle, and poor Charles standing miserably on the bar behind my mother, holding on for all he was worth. I found it very hard work pounding away on my hard tyres; a glorious, but not a pleasurable pastime.

Then one day at lunch, my father said he had just seen a new kind of tyre, filled up with air, and he thought it might be a success. And soon after that everyone had bicycles, ladies and all; and bicycling became the smart thing in Society, and the lords and ladies had their pictures in the papers, riding along in the park, in straw boater hats. We were then promoted to wearing baggy knicker bockers under our frocks, and over our white frilly drawers. We thought this horridly improper, but rather grand; . . . I only once saw a woman (not, of course, a lady) in real bloomers. (62)

Ways of getting about London were becoming more varied and also more dangerous:

In London, as elsewhere, there are different classes of travellers, and various modes of locomotion; the classes may be broadly divided into the residential, the business, and the pleasure travellers; and the modes of locomotion, into the pedestrian, by steam boat, by railway, by cabs and other spring carriages; and by omnibuses, including tramway cars, and the omnibus that now plies daily under the Thames.

London pedestrians run the risk, as about fifty to one, of being run over in the streets, that they do of being killed by railway accident. (63)

There was talk of building a tunnel under the English Channel, but many people disagreed with the idea. Here is part of a letter written in 1882 (the tunnel has still not been built!)

Here Mr. Knowles has come in, in a perfect storm of terror about the tunnel under the Channel . . . he is persuaded that 20,000 soldiers will be able to force their way through, all ours are in Ireland, England is no longer an island, and tho' as Britannia able to rule the waves she could not manage the tunnels. Mr. Chamberlain has some dreamy notions of universal brotherhood, we are to form one of the United States of Europe and the Board of Trade will be the great power amongst them. (64)

An entirely new kind of road travel was available to rich and adventurous people at the end of the century. Here is an advertisement:

Fifteen reasons why

AN AUTOCAR

is better than a horse-drawn vehicle:

BECAUSE

1. It wants no stable—the coach-house is enough.
2. It needs no daily grooming, consequently
3. No man need be kept specially to look after it.
4. There is no manure heap to poison the air.
5. It cannot shy, kick, or run away.
6. It has no will of its own to thwart the wishes of its driver and cause disaster.
7. It is more absolutely under control than any horse.
8. It costs nothing to keep, and cannot 'eat its head off in the stable.'
9. It consumes only when working, and then in exact proportion to the work done.
10. It cannot fall sick and die.
11. It will do more work than any two horses, and
12. Will travel twice as fast as any one.
13. It can be stopped with certainty and safety in half the distance.
14. No cruelty is inflicted by climbing a steep hill with a full load.
15. Nor can distress be caused by high-speed travelling.

(65)

An efficient postal service was operating and people no longer paid according to the distance a letter was to travel, as had been the custom. The Royal Kalendar *reported on August 9, 1870:*

From 1st October 1870, there may be sent by post between

places in the United Kingdom, at the rate of one halfpenny—
(1) a postcard, (2) a book packet, or pattern, or sample
packet, not exceeding 2 oz. in weight, (3) a registered newspaper. (66)

*At the Great Exhibition in 1851 there was a wonderful new machine
displayed. Queen Victoria wrote in her Journal on July 9th:*

We went to the Exhibition and had the electric telegraph
show explained and demonstrated before us. It is the most
wonderful thing, and the boy who worked it does so with the
greatest ease and rapidity. (67)

Other marvels followed and were reported in the newspapers: Punch,
in 1877:

"On putting the instrument (the telephone) to my ear, I felt
somewhat as if a regiment of the line had fired a volley, at a
hundred yards, into that member." (68)

The Times, *September 1879:*

"We publish in another column the extraordinary new uses
of which this invention (the telephone) has been found capable.
By its means the human voice can be conveyed in full force
from any one point to any other five miles off, and with some
loss of power to a very much more considerable distance
still." (69)

The Westminster Gazette, *December 12, 1896:*

Mr. W. H. Preece, the telegraphic expert of the Post Office,
had a surprise in store for his audience at Toynbee Hall on
Saturday night, when he lectured on, "Telegraphy without
Wires." . . . Towards the end of his lecture he announced that
a Mr. Marconi, a young Italian electrician, came to him
recently with a system of telegraphy without wires, depending
. . . on electric waves . . . of a vibration (of) 250,000,000 a
second. These vibrations were projected through space in
straight lines. . . .

Mr. Marconi was present that night, and this was the first
occasion on which the apparatus had been shown, except to
the Government officials. (70)

In 1867 Punch *reported a new discovery:*

"Writing superseded. Mr. Pratt, of Alabama, is the inventor

of a typewriting machine, lately exhibited to the London Society of Arts, which is said to print a man's thoughts twice as fast as he can write them with the present process. By a sort of piano arrangement the letters are brought in contact with carbonized paper, which is moved by the same manipulation.

(71)

Towns and Buildings

(See the pictures on pp. 39–47.)

In the seventeenth and eighteenth centuries only one great architectural style had been appreciated in England—that of classical Greece and Rome. In the nineteenth century the architecture of the Middle Ages was rediscovered and greatly valued. This resulted in a rivalry which was known as the Battle of the Styles.

Very few architects and designers thought about the need for a new, truly nineteenth-century style, suited to the new industrial society, and you will see that all the buildings illustrated in this book are copies or adaptations of one or another past style.

Towns were growing rapidly and living conditions in the poorer districts were very bad indeed. Charles Dickens was one of many people who protested at the lack of sanitation. Here is part of a letter which he wrote in 1854:

. . . they never will save their children from the dreadful and unnatural mortality now prevalent among them (almost too murderous to be thought of), or save themselves from untimely sickness and death, until they have cheap pure water in unlimited quantity, wholesome air, constraint upon little landlords . . . to keep their property decent under the heaviest penalties, efficient drainage and such alterations in building acts as shall preserve open spaces in the closest regions, and make them where they are not now. That a worthless Government which is afraid of every little interest and trembles before the vote of every dust contractor, will never do these things for them or pay the least sincere attention to them, until they are made election questions and the working-people unite to express their determination to have them, or to keep out of Parliament by every means in their power, every man who turns his back upon these first necessities. . . . I clearly see . . .

that nothing will have been done when the cholera comes again. Let it come twice again, severely,—the people advancing all the while in the knowledge that humanly speaking, it is, like Typhus Fever in the mass, a preventible disease—and you will see such a shake in this country as never was seen on Earth since Samson pulled the Temple down upon his head.

(72)

One of the improvements which Dickens suggested was that larger houses should be built. Compare his reasons with those given nowadays in favour of flats:

It is a very good thing to try several descriptions of houses, but I have no doubt myself (after long consideration of the subject) that the large houses are best. You never can, for the same money, offer anything like the same advantages in small houses. It is *not* desirable to encourage any small carpenter or builder who has a few pounds to invest, to run up small dwelling houses. If they had been discouraged long ago, London would be an immeasurably healthier place than it can be made in scores of years to come. If you go into any common outskirts of the town now and see the advancing army of brick and mortar laying waste the country fields and shutting out the air, you cannot fail to be struck by the consideration that if large buildings had been erected for the working people, instead of the absurd and expensive walnut shells in which they live, London would have been about a third of its present size, and every family would have had a country walk miles nearer to their own door. Besides this, men would have been nearer to their work—would not have had to dine at public houses—there would have been thicker walls of separation and better means of separation than you can ever give (except at a preposterous cost) in small tenements—and they would have had gas, water, drainage, and a variety of other humanizing things which you *can't* give them so well in little houses. Further, in little houses, you must keep them near the ground, and you cannot by any possibility afford such sound and wholesome foundations (remedying this objection) in little houses as in large ones. The example of large houses appears

105

to me, in all respects (always supposing their locality to be a great place like London) far better than any example you can set by small houses; and the compensation you give for any overgrown shadow they may cast upon a street at certain hours of the day is out of all proportion to that drawback. (73)

A Frenchman who visited England in 1871 wrote:

. . . street boys abound—bare-footed, dirty, and turning wheels in order to get alms. On the stairs leading to the Thames they swarm, more pale-faced, more deformed, more repulsive than the scum of Paris; without question, the climate is worse, and the gin more deadly. Near them, leaning against the greasy walls, or inert on the steps, are men in astounding rags; it is impossible to imagine before seeing them how many layers of dirt an overcoat or a pair of trousers could hold; they dream or doze openmouthed, their faces are begrimed, dull, and sometimes streaked with red lines. It is in these localities that families have been discovered with no other bed than a heap of soot; they had slept there during several months. For a creature so wasted and jaded there is but one refuge— drunkenness . . . A trader said to me, "Look after your pockets, sir," and a policeman warned me not to enter certain lanes. (74)

It was in 1887 that Trafalgar Square and the Embankment, in London, first became haunts of the homeless poor. Before this, many wealthy people had had no idea that there were people living in such conditions:

Just as Big Ben strikes two, the moon, flashing across the Thames and lighting up the stone-work of the Embankment, brings into relief a pitiable spectacle. Here on the stone abutments, which afford a slight protection from the biting wind, are scores of men lying side by side, huddled together for warmth, and, of course, without any other covering than their ordinary clothing, which is scanty enough at the best. Some have laid down a few pieces of waste-paper, by way of taking the chill off the stones, but the majority are too tired even for that, and the nightly toilet of most consists of first removing the hat, swathing the head in whatever rag may be doing duty as a handkerchief, and then replacing the hat. (75)

Towns near coalfields and at river mouths were spreading rapidly:

Barrow . . . has swelled almost within the memory of the youngest inhabitant from the quiet coast-nest of some five score fishermen into the busy, bustling, blazing, money-making, money-spending, roaring, tearing, swearing, steaming, sweltering seat of twenty thousand iron workers, and the crime and culture, the dirt and disease, the hard-working and hard-drinking, the death and life, the money and misery they bring along with them!

Barrow . . . holds a Monster-Iron-Mining-and-Smelting Company, with two Dukes among its directors, to say nothing of Lord knows who, in the way of Lords, and Lord knows how many millionaires! (76)

By 1871, there were already suggestions about better town-planning:

I know nothing more disheartening and unwise . . . than our system of mean and narrow suburban roads. . . . A broad and pleasant tree-planted road through such a district would, by opening it up and making it attractive to the inhabitants of London in general, prove as beneficial from a commercial as from a sanitary and an aesthetic point of view. (77)

Trade and Industry

(See the pictures on pp. 48–57.)

Trade was greatly helped by the Great Exhibition which was held in Hyde Park in 1851. The Prince Consort said that it would be "a living picture of the point of development at which mankind has arrived," but there was a great deal of argument about the site and the building. Joseph Paxton, who had been gardener to the Duke of Devonshire, designed a huge glasshouse and people came flocking from all over this country and abroad to see it. People were anxious to possess the kinds of things they saw there and the Exhibition had a great effect upon public taste. Queen Victoria showed much interest and visited the site in February, three months before the Exhibition opened. She wrote in her diary:

1851. February 18. . . . drove to look at the Crystal Palace, which really now is one of the wonders of the world, which we English may indeed be proud of. . . . The galleries are finished, and from the top of them the effect is quite wonderful. The sun shining in through the Transept gave a fairy-like appearance. The building is so light and graceful, in spite of its immense size. Many of the Exhibits have arrived, . . . (78)

1851. April 29. We drove to the Exhibition . . . and remained about 2 hours and ½. . . . We went up into the Gallery, and the sight of it from there into all the Courts, full of all sorts of objects of art, manufacture, etc. had quite the effect of fairyland. The noise was tremendous, as there was so much going on, of all kinds and sorts, and at least 12 to 20,000 engaged in work of every kind. The collection of raw materials is very fine. The clocks, and articles of silver, stuffs, English ribbons lace etc. are beautiful. Indeed it shows of what immense use to this Country this Exhibition is, as it goes to prove we are capable of doing almost anything. We went down and examined the French part, in which there are the most exquisite things . . . Looked also at the Italian, Spanish, Portuguese and German parts. The Austrian section is nearly finished, and beautiful. There are very splendid exhibits in porcelain and iron, from Berlin, lovely embroideries from Switzerland etc. . . . Russia is far behind as the ships were frozen in and could not bring the things sooner. . . . (79)

May 7 . . . to the Exhibition remaining there nearly 2 hours. . . . We went to the Courts allotted to Tunis and China, which are very interesting, and Tunis particularly beautiful, being arranged as a native bazaar, full of magnificent embroideries, stuffs, metal work, etc., and the blending of colours exquisite. In all these compartments there are likewise the *raw* products, dried fruits, perfumery, in fact everything that can be made in each country. From here we crossed the Transept to where the Indian exhibits were placed. We were quite dazzled by the most splendid shawls and tissues. Next went to South Australia and New Zealand, where the exhibits consist chiefly of raw products—but very valuable ones, such as beautiful specimens of wood etc. Canada made an admirable show, fine furniture, pretty sledges, and a very good and novel kind of fire engine. We then went into the Sculpture Court, containing many fine pieces. . . . After this to Mr. Pugin's mediaeval room, full of church ornaments, beautiful mantlepieces etc. and lastly through a collection of furniture, lamps, ornaments of the most novel and tasteful kind from Birmingham. . . . (80)

All the most famous people were there when the Queen opened the Exhibition on May 1, 1851. One lady wrote in her diary:

. . . At length a rumour was heard that the Queen was in the building, and precisely as the clock struck twelve she issued from the waiting room . . . and accompanied by Prince Albert and the two eldest children, proceeded to her place amidst the uncontrolled enthusiasm of the multitudes of people. It was a noble sight; she stood on the raised dais, in front of the Chair of State on which she sat not, even for a moment. Her husband and her children were beside her, her Court immediately about her. Around her, the highest names of England, and thousands less renowned but no less loyal; and all this pomp and panoply were called together to do honour to the industry of millions, whose toils, erst scorned upon, seemed suddenly ennobled. It was a proud moment for our Queen, for England! While the nations of the earth were convulsed, she has called into existence this peaceful meeting, the most gigantic ever known. . . . As the wife of the largest manufacturer in the world, I could not but feel this to be a most impressive sight, . . . the most dazzling sight I ever beheld; grander even than Her coronation in our glorious Abbey. (81)

At this period we were often referred to as a "nation of shop-keepers." The following letter tells of the founding of one of London's big stores:

It is interesting to recall Whiteley's humble beginning. . . . I discovered that (my mother) had found a most serviceable little shop newly opened in Westbourne Grove where she had got into the habit of doing all her shopping for small things. Many years later Mr. Whiteley told us much about that little shop.

When it was opened by him and one assistant, their first customer was an old Scotch lady. Shrewdly taking in at a glance how new everything looked, she asked the assistant how long they had been open. "Only since this morning," he informed her; "and you are our first customer!" added Mr. Whiteley. Whereupon the old lady, having completed her purchases, suggested, "Let us ask God's blessing on this enterprise and pray for your success!" So they all knelt down on the floor while the old lady offered up a prayer! . . .

(John Barker was an employee of Whiteley. When Sir James Whitehead consulted Whiteley as to the best investment for a sum of money, he suggested the establishment of a linen-draper's shop in a good neighbourhood. Whiteley recommended John Barker as a suitable man to run such a business.) (82)

Working conditions in the factories were still very bad and hours of work intolerably long. Many people tried to improve matters but others objected to any suggestion of laws which would "interfere" with trade. Here are four bad cases of the employment of children:

Lord Brougham . . . brought before the Lords the case of the young children employed in Bleach Works. It is a cruel one. Infants of seven or eight years old are at work for eighteen hours, and are sometimes four nights without sleep. The brutalities by which the poor little children are kept sufficiently awake for the purposes of their task-masters are shocking. *1860.*
(83)

From the evidence of Mr. Ruff a master sweep of Nottingham, before a Royal Commission in 1864:

No one knows the cruelty a boy has to undergo in learning. The flesh must be hardened. This must be done by rubbing it, chiefly on the elbows and knees, with the strongest brine, close by a hot fire. You must stand over them with a cane, or coax them by a promise of a half-penny, if they will stand a few more rubs. At first they will come back from their work streaming with blood, and the knees looking as if the caps had been pulled off. Then they must be rubbed with brine again. (84)

Lord Lyttelton . . . gave an instance of:

. . . a little girl engaged in a brickyard near Birmingham from 6 a.m. to 8 p.m., only having fifteen minutes for breakfast, and thirty minutes for dinner, no time for tea, and during one day she would have to catch and throw to her neighbour fifteen tons of bricks. *About 1867.* (85)

From a report to the Town Council of Sheffield, 1867:

A boy, only nine years old, . . . was obliged by his father to work as cellar-boy in one of the furnaces, on most days of the week from six in the morning to six or seven in the evening, and on Saturdays from three in the morning till three in the afternoon. This enforced labour at a high temperature would, if only occasional, appear to be equivalent to a somewhat long compulsory innings in the Turkish bath. (86)

Here is a typical story, showing something of the working conditions even in the West End of London:

Public indignation has been excited by the accounts of the death of Mary Anne Walkley, a girl employed by Madame Elise, of Regent Street, . . . a notorious dressmaker. "Long hours in an overcrowded room and sleeping in an ill-ventilated bedroom," said Sir George Grey, "caused the young girl's death." . . . Lord Shaftesbury in the Lords, and Mr. Bagwell in the Commons, called attention to the system under which such girls are killed; . . . (87)

Working conditions in the new industrial towns were described by a famous Churchman, writing to his wife in April 1883:

We walked over mounds of dirt in which fowls pecked but on which no grass would grow. The streams were foetid and slimy, the paths were unkept, and lying about were brick stones, broken implements, and garbage. Many of the houses were in ruins and some disused chimneys were left to fall. It was not the ugliness of poverty but of wealth; everyone was too well off to care for a bit of grass, too busy to tidy up, too anxious to move to new quarters to care for the old. We went through the plate-rolling works; it was magnificent to see the power of the men who tossed about the burning plates; but with the thought of the country around, I surprised Bolton by an outbreak against civilization.

"What is the good of progress if it makes the condition of life so bare for the many that a few may have luxuries? What change has been brought about but a great increase of population?" (88)

Some firms were more enlightened and provided good conditions for their workpeople. Here is an account of a visit to Bournville in 1897:

Such a factory!—dressing-rooms for the girls in which to change into white, bath-rooms, dining-rooms, heated and ventilated work-rooms, open spaces, and gardens between the workshops, about 2,000 employed. But, best of all, a model village in which every tree on the ground was preserved, a coppice left for shelter, and a playground within three minutes of every child. (89)

Throughout three-quarters of the nineteenth century Britain was called "The workshop of the world" and our industries had no rivals. Gradually, however, other countries were becoming industrialized and there were many warnings, like this one written in 1887:

At this moment we are engaged in a struggle, which to a mind so trained and unprejudiced as that of Professor Huxley is indistinguishable from a state of war, with Germany, Italy, France and with the United States, to say nothing of the small states of Europe, for the command of the markets of the world. We have no longer the monopoly of the great industries. Mulhausen competes with Manchester, and Liège with Sheffield. (90)

Crime and Punishment

The bad living conditions in the towns were certainly the greatest cause of crime and many men and women did what they could to improve housing. Reformatories of various kinds were started by voluntary effort. In 1853 Joseph Sturge, a Quaker, had founded a Reformatory Institution in Birmingham. He reported:

I used to go and sit with them (the lads in the Reformatory) for two or three hours a day, and I used to tell them that they might, by governing their tongues, their tempers and their appetites, and governing themselves generally, be much more happy. . . . and I showed them how wrong it was to break the social laws that bind society together, and also the laws of God, and so forth. I considered that my conversation with them for two or three hours had had a great effect; and I provided them with wholesome food, and I gave them clothes to wear, and I surrounded them with as many comforts as I possibly could. (91)

Conditions were so bad in 1857 that more and more people had begun to urge that Parliament should take some steps to improve things. Notice one of the cures that was suggested:

We have to look back upon a year stained beyond all precedent with frightful crimes of every sort and kind: horrible murders, enormous frauds and scandalous robberies and defalcations. The whole attention of the country is now drawn to the social questions which press upon us with appalling urgency, and the next session of parliament . . . must be principally engaged in the endeavour to find remedies for the evils and dangers incident to our corrupted population, and our erroneous and inadequate penal system, the evils and dangers of which threaten to become greater and more difficult

114

to remedy every day. . . . At least we ought to make the experiment whether the diffusion of education will or will not be conducive to the diminution of crime. . . . (92)

People sent to prison were classified according to the kind of crime they had committed. This list of diets was suggested by a parliamentary committee in 1864. Diets were kept as low as possible, for it was feared that if prisoners were well fed then poor people might be attracted to crime!

			Class I	Class II	Class III	Class IV	Class V
			ozs.	ozs.	ozs.	ozs.	ozs.
Breakfast	Every day	Bread	6	6	8	8	8
		Gruel	—	1 pt.	1 pt.	1 pt.	1 pt.
Supper	Every day	Bread	6	6	6	8	8
		Gruel	—	—	1 pt.	1 pt.	1 pt.
Supper	Sundays	Bread	8	8	10	10	12
		Cheese	—	1	2	3	3
		Bread	6	6	4	4	4
	Mondays	Potatoes	—	—	12	16	16
Dinner	Wednesdays	Suet Pudding	—	—	8	12	12
	Fridays	Indian Meal Pudding	6	8	—	—	—
	Tuesdays	Bread	6	6	8	8	8
Dinner	Thursdays	Potatoes	8	12	8	8	16
	Saturdays	Soup	—	—	¾ pt.	1 pt.	1 pt.

Note. Hard Labour men to receive extra cheese, gruel and meat. (93)

Prison was regarded as mainly a punishment, not as a means of preventing crime, as this report issued in 1863 shows:

You may tell a man that he shall work so many turns (on the Crank—a form of hard labour) or have no breakfast, . . . so many turns or no dinner, or so many turns and no supper, but it was found that, first of all, there is something in the Saxon blood which every now and then rebels, and you cannot make a man work; then what are you to do? At Birmingham the food was withdrawn, and the men at last became so ill that some of them died. There was a great inquiry into the matter in a court of law, and . . . the governor was sentenced to three months' imprisonment. (94)

Punishments seem to us to have been out of all proportion to the crime committed, as this story shows:

On going into the next cell, we found another prisoner, aged about forty-five years, a cabman, who told us a very doleful story. He had been intrusted with a chest of tea by some party unknown to convey in his cab to a particular place in the metropolis. He supposes the police were after the man who had hired him, as he made his escape immediately after he had given the property into his custody. For the unlawful possession of this chest of tea, he had received a sentence of twelve months' imprisonment with hard labour. He has a wife and family, for whom he appeared to be much concerned. (95)

Executions took place in public until 1868 and many people protested that this custom was degrading and harmful. Here is a letter written to The Times *by Charles Dickens:*

I was a witness of the execution at Horsemonger-lane this morning. I went there with the intention of observing the crowd gathered to behold it. . . . A sight so inconceivably awful as the wickedness and levity of the immense crowd . . . could be imagined by no man, . . . The horrors of the gibbet and of the crime which brought the wretched murderers to it, faded in my mind before the atrocious bearing, looks and language, of the assembled spectators.

. . . When the day dawned, thieves, low prostitutes, ruffians, and vagabonds of every kind, flocked on to the ground, with every variety of offensive and foul behaviour. . . . When the sun rose brightly . . . it gilded thousands upon thousands of upturned faces, so inexpressibly odious in their brutal mirth or callousness, that a man had cause . . . to shrink from himself, as fashioned in the image of the Devil. When the two miserable creatures who attracted all this ghastly sight . . . were turned quivering into the air, there was no more emotion, no more pity, . . . no more restraint in any of the previous obscenities than if the name of Christ had never been heard in the world, and there were no belief among men but that they perished like beasts.

. . . I do not believe that any community can prosper where

such a scene of horror and demoralization . . . is presented at the very doors of good citizens, and is passed by, unknown or forgotten. (96)

Here is a vivid description of a visit to Portland, on Sunday, August 20, 1882:

. . . drove up to the prison standing at the top of the cliff and went to church with about 1400 convicts. They are divided into companies, shut off from each other by strong partitions in squares, each square guarded by armed warders on raised seats. A small body of soldiers ready to fire under the gallery, a most terrible sight: their behaviour was most impressive, the great quiet, nobody coughed or fidgeted, all seemed deeply attending, and hymns and chants were joined in with immense vigour. The organist was a murderer. One man who had lately killed his jailer was separated and guarded by himself. The sermon rather poor, . . . Went all over the place, the cells, kitchen, laundry, punishment cells, etc., and dining perhaps the most striking of all. A loaf and cheese stood on the floor in front of 250 cells. At the word of command the doors opened as if by magic and 250 convicts stood on the thresholds. "Pick up yr. dinners." They all stooped. "Back to yr. cells. Shut yr. doors," and with a crash of thunder they all vanished, and every door was double locked. They may never speak to each other. They lose all identity and are only known by their numbers written on their backs. There has never been a successful escape, though many marvellous and miraculous attempts. The great difficulty to contend with is laziness. One man has preferred punishments, i.e. living on bread and water, for 3 years rather than hard labour. He has slept the whole of the time, day and night, except during the one hour's solitary exercise. Flogging has had the best effect of all. . . . The death rate extraordinarily small. (97)

Government

This was a time of great changes in people's lives in Britain, yet on the whole there was social peace and increasing prosperity. In most countries of Europe great social conflicts broke into political revolution in the nineteenth century, but in England both parties—Liberals and Conservatives—favoured peaceful progress and social reform.

Yet England was certainly not a democratic country, if by that we mean a country where the people, by their votes, decide what is to happen. Only very gradually, in three Reform Acts, was the right to vote granted to more and more people. In 1865 the following were NOT allowed to vote. (Notice how foolish some of these omissions appear to us, yet a great many serious and intelligent people argued that they were sensible and right):

Women; persons under twenty-one years of age; peers; Irish peers except members of the House of Commons; aliens, unless made denizens by the Queen's letters patent, or naturalized by Act of Parliament; persons of unsound mind—idiots and lunatics; persons convicted of felony, bribery, perjury, or petit larceny; commissioners and officers of excise, customs, stamps and taxes; all persons in the employ of the post office; police magistrates or police officers, and all persons employed in the Thames and Metropolitan police, and in the counties of Hertford, Essex, Kent, Surrey and Middlesex. (98)

Before 1872 voting was "open":

. . . the voter presented himself at the polling-booth, was asked his name and for which candidate he voted. It is obvious that this gave a great scope for intimidation and undue influence . . . In 1871 Mr. Forster, then Vice-President of the Council, introduced and carried through the House of Commons a Bill which would establish (the Ballot) by law . . . the

House of Lords resisted, and the measure was thrown out, only to be reintroduced next year and carried after many months had been wasted in unnecessary wrangling . . . the Lords . . . inserted a clause limiting it to eight years; but experience soon showed the advantages of this method of voting to be so considerable that the measure for its renewal was passed almost without a protest. (99)

Although on the whole both Liberals and Conservatives pursued very similar policies when they were in power, there was a deep division between them as to whether or not Ireland should be allowed to break away from Great Britain and have her own Parliament. Mr. Gladstone fought vigorously for the "Home Rule" Bill. Here are two extracts from his daughter's diary:

London, Thurs. 8 Ap. (1886) . . . to see the reception (of Mr. Gladstone) outside the House. The rain came down in torrents, but above the storm and above the roar of London thrilled the cheers, all the way from Downing Street we heard them . . . flew up the 200 steps to the gallery and saw the splendid reception there. The starting to their feet of the M.P.'s, the wonderful cheers. . . . for 3 hours and ½ he spoke—the most quiet earnest pleading, explaining, analysing, showing a mastery of detail. . . . Not a sound was heard, not a cough even, only cheers breaking out here and there . . . (100)

Hawarden, Tues. June 8 (1886). Woke early and wondered. At 8, came letters, one from the P.M. ending with these fateful words: "To-night is a great night. The odds are against our bill. The loss of it, if it comes, will be an unmixed mischief, postponing, not altering, the final issue." . . . the bill was lost, 30 majority against . . . (101)

Local Government was brought up to date by an Act of 1888. Here are extracts from a Handbook explaining the Act:

Mr. Ritchie's new Act may be described as the first step in the development of a simple, systematic and popular form of local government throughout England and Wales. It owes its origin to a two-fold demand—for more democratic institutions in our country districts, and for greater simplicity in our local authorities and areas.

In the first place, it has long been felt by practical politicians, that any re-modelling of our county government must involve the establishment of popularly-elected boards, directly representing the general body of the ratepayers. The rule of the county justices (owing chiefly, no doubt, to its admitted efficiency, economy and freedom from corruption), has long survived that of all other non-elected administrative bodies. In these days, when every householder has a right to vote for his representative, both in the town councils of municipal boroughs and in the National Parliament, it is clear that, if extended powers and increased grants of public money are to be given to county authorities, they can only be put into the hands of a council elected on a broad and popular suffrage.

. . . from a practical point of view still more pressing, is the demand for simplification . . . local government in England . . . is defective, complex and chaotic in the highest degree. This is partly the result of natural growth and decay, partly of recent legislation. Much of the ancient system of parish and manor, hundred and shire, which of old made England the fatherland of free institutions, has now grown obsolete, and unsuited to present social conditions. (102)

Religion

The new scientific ideas of men like Darwin and Huxley led many people to doubt whether everything in the Bible was literally true, and so set up a conflict in England between science and religion. But the majority of people still held firm beliefs about the truth of the Bible, and about the importance of frequent prayers and of regular church-going. Here is a description of the religious teaching in a well-to-do family:

Our father was the most cheerful of companions, loving to take us about to any kind of sights or entertainments which offered, and buying us toys and presents on every possible occasion. The only constraint put upon us, . . . concerned religious observance. We had to come in to daily Prayers at 10 o'clock, even if it interfered with working in our gardens or other outdoor amusement—and church twice on Sundays was the invariable rule as soon as we were old enough to walk to the neighbouring village. . . . We had to learn some "Scripture lesson" every day and two or three on Sundays, and I being the eldest had not only to repeat these Sunday lessons to my mother, but also to see . . . that my younger brothers and sisters knew theirs. I was made to learn any number of chapters and hymns, and Scripture catechisms—not to speak of the Thirty-nine Articles! (103)

There were many vigorous groups both in the Church of England and among Nonconformists at this time. Here is a description of a service taken by a famous Nonconformist preacher:

I am just come from hearing the celebrated Mr. Spurgeon preach . . . he told us from the pulpit that 9,000 people were present. The service was like the Presbyterian: Psalms, prayers, expounding a psalm, and a sermon. He is certainly very remarkable, and undeniably a very fine character: not remarkable in person, . . . a very clear and powerful voice, which was heard through the whole hall; a manner natural, impassioned, and without affectation or extravagance; wonderful fluency and command of language, . . . but without anything either ridiculous or irreverent. He gave me an impression of his earnestness and his sincerity, speaking without book or notes, yet his discourse was evidently very carefully prepared. . . . He preached for about three-quarters of an hour, and, to judge of the handkerchiefs and the audible sobs, with great effect.

(104)

Church activities were very varied and most people carried out their religious beliefs in practical ways:

Just as in the Church of England each parish in a large town tends to include in it a group of various agencies for both spiritual and social good, so the Nonconformist churches of large towns tend to be centres of great activity. To take one typical case, round the Congregational church known as Union Chapel, Islington, cluster a Benevolent Society, a Dorcas Society, a Maternity Society, a Tract Society, a Ministers' Aid Society, a Penny Bank, a Sunday school with nearly 700 scholars, and in connection with it a Sunday-school Institute or Guild for the elder scholars, a "Band of Hope" or Temperance Society for the young; there are organized branches of the missionary and other societies, the London Missionary Society, the Evangelical Continental Society, the Colonial Missionary and Irish Evangelical Societies, the Congregational Chapel Building Society, and the Jews Society; and there are two groups of branch institutions, chapels and missionaries, ragged schools and other benevolent agencies, which are supported and managed by the church in the East End of London. (105)

Gradually, less and less time was given to reading the Bible and religious books, to religious discussion and argument, and even to going to Church. Here is a letter written by a clergyman in 1878:

Somehow Sunday must be rescued from its present degradation, saved from being a day of sleep, feasting, and working, to become a day of learning, enjoyment, and rest . . . I try to blend with the other good influences of Sunday, the good influence of music, so that all may work together to give to the people fullness of life.

On two Sunday evenings in December Herr Franke gave classical concerts in our schoolroom (in Whitechapel). . . . There was a large demand for tickets which were freely given, and it need hardly be said that the music was perfect of its kind, very unlike any commonly heard in these parts. It seemed, though, entirely to capture the minds of the audience, and during some of the difficult pieces there was not a movement in the room.

I explained that I was introducing the music in no irreligious spirit, but simply because I believed such music would in the truest sense help the people to be religious. (106)

People were coming to admit that others were entitled to their religious beliefs:

Even within the last twenty years a Nonconformist was ineligible for almost all University emoluments; he might be compelled to contribute towards the working expenses of the church from which he dissented; and he could not bury his dead, except with rites which were distasteful to him, in a public churchyard.

With regard to religious bodies . . . the tendency has been towards their complete equality before the law. The Established Church remains established, but many of its exclusive privileges have been withdrawn. Compulsory Church rates . . . were finally abolished in 1868. Three years later . . . religious tests were abolished at the Universities. . . . The Jews were admitted to Parliament under the Jewish Disabilities Act of 1858: . . .
(107)

But many people were very concerned that people seemed now to be less enthusiastic about their religion and even to know less about it:

. . . every religious body has displayed great and unprece-dented activity in building churches, and in developing other elements of its organization; . . . the clergy of every denomina-tion have shown a devotion and a spirit of self-sacrifice beyond all praise; . . . the tone of religious controversy has softened . . . but, . . . has it (religion) touched the life, the habits, the

123

thoughts of the majority of the workmen in the great towns? Assuredly not: (108)

We call ourselves a Christian people and pride ourselves upon being a civilized nation. These two girls have said that they could neither read nor write; that they had never in their lives been at school, church or chapel; that they had never heard of the Bible; and . . . in all probability they had never heard of a Divine Being. We send out missionaries to the heathen, but what avails all this when we see such a state of things at home? (109)

The Empire

(See the pictures on page 58.)

At the beginning of Queen Victoria's reign the population of the British colonies, not including India, was about four million. In 1887 a writer pointed out how greatly emigration had increased during fifty years:

. . . the population of the British possessions other than the Indian Empire, is now some 16,000,000, of which considerably more than half are of British race. Besides this, there has been during the reign of the Queen, an extension, a consolidation, and a settlement of the vast Indian Empire, which of itself would mark this period as among the most important that English history has ever seen. (110)

Conditions in Australia were, by now, very different from what they had been early in the century, when prisoners were deported to New South Wales, often for quite small offences, and had to start their life anew in desperate circumstances.

At the end of the century a lady described the life of well-to-do Australians as she had experienced it during the 1860s:

Quite rich people, having . . . lands and flocks bringing in thousands a year, would have only three or four servants—the daughters of the house would do much of the work, and visitors would be quite prepared to help in making butter and cakes. A good deal that had been said in England about the splendid times which servants had overseas struck me on nearer observation as capable of being looked at from quite another point of view. For instance, much was made at one time of maid-servants having horses to ride. When the nearest town was perhaps fifteen or twenty miles off, when a horse cost £5 or £10, was never groomed, and when the rider himself or herself caught and saddled him as wanted, riding was not such an exceptional privilege.

Again it was true that wages were about double what they were in England, but accommodation was much rougher, and servants were expected to help in every department as required —no question of saying "that is not my place." (111)

In New Zealand there was for a time bitter fighting between the Maoris and British settlers, but the rich lands and warm climate continued to attract Englishmen and their families. Here are extracts from a list of applicants for immigration to New Zealand:

Name of Applicants Approved	*Remarks*
George Wain and wife	Are both healthy and respectable.
Sarah Ann Webb (Mrs. Catchpool will undertake to assist Sarah Webb until she joins her brother in the colony.)	Has an irreproachable character from the minister Mr. Copley—is very respectable in appearance and manner —is robust and healthy; has promised to join her brother who is gone out on the *Cuba*. The remainder of the family will follow next year if accounts are favourable.
William Welch and wife with 7 children (2 boys, 4 girls, 1 infant.)	A strong healthy couple. Have an excellent character from their late employer; the 2 eldest girls can milk and make butter—the eldest boy works occasionally—the education of the children has been well attended to. All are remarkably healthy and robust. All except the youngest have been vaccinated, had the whooping cough and measles. Welch has such a perfect general knowledge of all kinds of out-of-door labour that I consider him one of the best of his class I have yet met with. He will pay for the 6 children under age.

William Barker (Engaged by E. B. H. & Co.)	Of good character, an excellent general workman—understands smith's work in general, also shoeing, brazing and tin work. Is robust and healthy.
Applicants Rejected	
Francis Doughty	Single, pretended blacksmith—unfit for a colony—very dirty and very poor and illiterate.
William Horton, wife and family	Is given to drinking and unable to pay the childrens' passage. (112)

Even during the wars New Zealand was becoming a rich land of sheep-rearers. In 1882 the first refrigerator ship carrying New Zealand mutton sailed for England and since then "Canterbury Lamb" has become well known to English housekeepers. Here is an extract from a survey of the British food position at the time:

The home meat supply is only sufficient for seven and a half months out of the twelve, . . . An export trade of frozen meat has been opened from New Zealand. . . . The number of sheep in the colony has increased from 1½ million in 1858 to 14 million in 1884. (113)

Luxuries had for long been brought to England from India. In 1859 there was a report in The Times, *of London, of a new development:*

The Tea Tree in India. Mr. Henry Mann, an enterprising gentleman who left China about five years ago, has introduced the tea tree to Southern India, . . . The plantation is situated at an elevation of 6,000 feet, . . . and contains about 6,000 plants. The ground occupied is about four acres. The forest land is found most suitable for the plants. It now only remains to test the leaf and to procure skilled manufacturers. . . . The cultivation of tea in the hill districts of India seems to be spreading fast, and as these are the localities recommended for European colonization, we may yet see India rivalling China in this trade, and sturdy Anglo-Saxon pickers depicted on the tea chests instead of almond-eyed long-tailed men of China. (114)

India came under the direct government of the Crown after the Mutiny of 1857, but conditions there varied greatly:

127

Let me take you first to the great city of Calcutta. . . . You will meet native gentlemen who speak English as well as yourselves, who are ready to discuss with you English history and literature, modern philosophy and European politics. But, if you wander for a few miles into the surrounding country, . . . the first man you meet would hardly know the name of the Queen; he certainly could not tell you who was the Viceroy of India, and if he knew the name of the Lieutenant-Governor of Bengal, his immediate lord and master, it would be surprising. (115)

The west coast of Africa had for long been useful to Englishmen trading in slaves, but after the abolition of the slave trade in 1807 there was very little trade there, except in ivory and gold dust. In 1856 a new trade was commented upon:

The palm-oil trade has been opened here, however, in the course of the last twenty years, and promises to be more important than both of the other two branches of commerce united. . . . The trade of the country is concentrated at the forts, and almost the whole of it passes through the hands of a few foreign residents. None but the most trivial duties are imposed either upon the imports or exports, and the trade is consequently free to all nations. The English have the largest share, the Americans the next, and the Dutch and French together have perhaps one-fourth of the whole. (116)

But even so far-seeing a man as Charles Dickens did not think that there was much future for English interests in Africa. In 1857 he wrote:

. . . Without at all disparaging Dr. Livingstone or in the least doubting his facts, I think however that his deductions must be received with great caution. The history of all African effort, hitherto, is a history of wasted European life, squandered European money, and blighted European hope—in which the generous English have borne a great share. That it would be a great thing to cultivate that cotton and be independent of America, no one can doubt; but I think that happy end, with all its attendant good results, must be sought in India. There are two tremendous obstacles in Africa; one, the climate; the other, the people. (117)

At the very end of the century British interest in South Africa was very great, and led us into a serious war against the Boers, the original Dutch settlers there. Opinion in this country was greatly divided about the rights and wrongs of the war. Many people were against the government's policy:

There is so much likeness between what we did with those colonists (the Americans) and what we are doing with the Boers. We are so superior, so rude, so irresponsible in the way we call others ignorant, liars, etc., etc. We may be a great people, but we are not a nice people. (118)

During the middle years of the century there was much discussion in England about French plans for cutting a canal which would link the Mediterranean Sea with the Indian Ocean. Most people were against the idea:

The Lords had a discussion about the Canal of the Future, that is to say, the impossible trench which M. Lesseps pretends to think he can cut through the Isthmus of Suez. The Government opinion upon the subject is, that if the Canal could be made, we ought not, for political reasons, to allow it, but that inasmuch as the Canal cannot be cut, . . . the wise course is to let the speculators ruin themselves and diddle the Pasha. This seems straightforward and benevolent enough. (119)

But the canal was built and when, in 1875, the Khedive of Egypt offered a large number of shares in the Canal for sale, Disraeli the Prime Minister, bought them for England. This had a great influence upon communications between this country and the colonies:

The roads of communication with India and Australia are greatly altered from what they were at the beginning of the reign (of Queen Victoria). Then the main highway was round the Cape of Good Hope; now not only is the Suez Canal open, but it has been largely brought under the control of England, already owner of Aden and Perim, by the purchase of the Canal shares. The occupation of Cyprus has the object of further strengthening this position, while the opening of the Canadian Pacific Railway affords a third route to the Australian colonies. (120)

The colonial possessions brought greater prosperity to Britain, but a number of people did not think that this should be the main purpose of an imperial power. In 1872 the novelist Anthony Trollope expressed views which only became fact much later, in the middle of the twentieth century:

We are called upon to rule them (the colonies)—as far as we do rule them, not for our glory, but for their happiness. If we keep them, we should keep them—not because they add prestige to the name of Great Britain, not because they are gems in our diadem, not in order that we may boast that the sun never sets on our dependencies, but because by keeping them we may assist them in developing their own resources. And when we part with them, as part with them we shall, let us do so with neither smothered jealousy nor open hostility, but with a proud feeling that we are sending a son out into the world able to take his place among men. (121)

The Fighting Forces

(See the pictures on pp. 59–61.)

In England this was an age of peace and security and the only wars we were involved in were outside Europe. Conditions in the Crimean War disturbed many people at home:
. . . a vast black dreary wilderness of mud, dotted with little lochs of foul water, and seamed by dirty brownish . . . streams . . . everywhere are strewed the carcasses of horses and miserable animals torn by dogs and smothered in mud. Vultures sweep over . . . in flocks . . .

It is over this ground, gained at last by great toil and exhaustion and loss of life on the part of the starving beasts of burden, that man and horse have to struggle . . . for some four or five miles with the hay and corn, the meat, the biscuit, the pork, which form the subsistence of our army. Every day this toil must be undergone . . . Horses drop exhausted on the road, . . . Men wade and plunge about, and stumble through the mud, . . . or sit down exhausted, pictures of dirt and woe unutterable. Sometimes . . . the overworked and sickly soldier is seized with illness . . . aid is all but hopeless and impossible . . . Why should not roads have been made? . . . Their formation would have saved many lives, and have spared our men much sickness and pain. (122)

In 1857 a new decoration for gallantry was first presented:
A very proud day in the year 1857, when sixty-two men of all ranks were decorated with the Victoria Cross for conspicuous gallantry and deeds of valour. . . . The Victoria Crosses . . . were made from the iron of captured Russian guns in the Crimea. The ceremony took place in Hyde Park . . . the time came for the chosen recipients of the honour to march on to the piece of ground that was reserved for them only—the

bravest men in the world. The cheering was tremendous as they appeared.

Queen Victoria rode on to the scene punctually at . . . 9.30 a.m. She was accompanied by Prince Albert and the two young princes, Edward and Albert, both mounted on handsome little ponies and dressed in plaids and Scotch caps. The Queen herself wore a scarlet habit with a gold sash across the bodice, her small hat having a gold band round the crown and a white feather. . . . she bent down and pinned the Victoria Cross on each man's breast, when he advanced to her horse's side. . . . The name of the man, and the deed of valour and daring by which he had earned it, was read out beforehand. . . . After all had been thus decorated, the V.C. heroes . . . formed up in line about fifty yards distant from the Queen, and in the space between the troops marched past with colours flying and bands playing. (123)

During Queen Victoria's reign conditions in the army improved greatly:

1. The . . . wars (in Afghanistan, China, India, etc.) taught us how foolish and cruel it was to feed men badly—that salt beef or pork and biscuit, with a strong dram of rum and a pinch of tea and sugar, were not enough for the British soldier to live on for any length of time. More recent campaigns have made it evident that money spent in providing our men with jam, pickles, cheese, bacon, preserved vegetables, etc. is well and economically expended.

2. . . . the loss from sunstroke and heat-apoplexy that resulted from the cruel habit of making our soldiers fight, even in the tropics, in leather stocks, tightly buttoned-up jackets, and without any effective protection from the sun on their heads. . . . A great deal still (1887) remains to be done before the soldier is clothed in a manner suitable for the life he has to lead in the field, and before we follow the example of the navy, and dress our men suitably for the hard work they have to do.

3. In fighting courage, marching power, endurance and physical strength the soldier of today (1887) is fully equal to his prototype who fought under Wellington. Thanks to his better education, he is now more intelligent, better disciplined,

far better behaved, more contented, and, indeed, in every way far more efficient for all the purposes for which he is maintained. As for the officers, they come still from the same class that has always furnished the army and navy with leaders, but they are more professional than formerly. (124)

Although men were no longer press-ganged into the navy, conditions there were still very bad. When Lord Fisher joined the navy in 1854, in the first ship he was in, fresh water was carried in casks and ship's biscuit was supplied in what was known as "bread bags." He wrote:

These bread-bags were not preservative; they were creative. A favourite amusement was to put a bit of this biscuit on the table and see how soon all of it would walk away. In fact one midshipman could gamble away his "tot" of rum with another midshipman by pitting one bit of biscuit against another. Anyhow, whenever you took a bit of biscuit to eat it you always tapped it edgeways on the table to let the 'grown-ups' get away. The water was nearly as bad as the biscuit. It was turgid—it was smelly—it was animally. (125)

By 1887 conditions had improved:

1. In deference to the public opinion of the country, flogging has been discontinued, and discipline is now enforced by a carefully framed scale of fines and mulcts and by a liberal and discriminating distribution of rewards.

2. . . . the introduction of a careful system of training for ships' cooks and the establishment of canteens in Her Majesty's ships deserve mention. (126)

Science and Invention

(See the pictures on pp. 62–64.)

In this period of great scientific and industrial development there were a number of writers and thinkers who were disturbed by the ways in which people's lives were changing. John Ruskin was one of these. In Modern Painters *he wrote:*

The great mechanical impulses of the age, of which most of us are so proud, are a mere passing fever, half-speculative, half-childish. People will discover at last that royal roads to anything can no more be laid in iron than they can in dust; that there are, in fact, no royal roads to anywhere worth going to; that if there were, it would that instant cease to be worth going to—I mean, so far as the things to be obtained are in any way estimable in terms of *price*. For there are two classes of precious things in the world: those that God gives us for nothing—sun, air, and life (both mortal life and immortal); and the secondarily precious things which He gives us for a price: these secondarily precious things, . . . can only be bought for definite money; they never can be cheapened. No cheating nor bargaining will ever get a single thing out of nature's "establishment" at half-price. Do we want to be strong?—we must work. . . . To be happy?—we must be kind. To be wise?—we must look and think. No changing of place at a hundred miles an hour, nor making of stuffs a thousand yards a minute, will make us one whit stronger, happier, or wiser. There was always more in the world than men could see, walked they ever so slowly; they will see it no better for going fast. And they will at last, and soon too, find out that their grand inventions for conquering (as they think) space and time, do, in reality, conquer nothing; for space and time . . . did not want any sort of conquering; they wanted *using*. A fool always wants to shorten space and time; a wise man wants to lengthen both. . . . Your railroad, when you come to understand it, is only a device for making the world smaller: and as for being able to talk from place to place, that is, indeed, well and convenient; but suppose you have, originally, nothing to say. We shall be obliged at last to confess, what we should long ago have known, that the really precious things are thought and sight, not pace. It does a bullet no good to go fast; and a man, if he be truly a man, no harm to go slow; for his glory is not at all in going, but in being. (127)

An English doctor, looking back on his work in hospitals, wrote at the end of the century:

I am fully aware of the great progress which has been made since the days when I was a student. It was while I was a student that the clinical thermometer . . . came into use; before that time everyone had to be content with . . . the feeling of the hot skin. . . .

The days when a test-tube, a spirit-lamp and an imperfect microscope supplied all the equipment needed (for studying diseases) have long passed away. Such an examination as the present state of science makes imperative can no longer be conducted in a corner behind a screen. It is today absolutely necessary . . . alike in the interests of the individual patient and for the well-being of mankind . . . that each hospital should be provided with laboratories, . . . fully equipped with all the needed appliances of sciences. . . . Our great hospitals in London are still very deficient in such an equipment. I venture to assert that in this respect our London hospitals in general are both absolutely behindhand and relatively in the rear of hospitals not only in other countries but even in our own provinces. (128)

Scientific invention was applied to many frivolous purposes, as well as many worthy ones. Here is something which you, yourself, might have found useful:

Registered Alarum Bedstead. By means of a common alarum-clock hung at the head of the bed, and adjusted in the usual way to go off at a desired hour, the front legs of the bedstead, immediately the alarum ceases ringing, are made to fold underneath, and the sleeper, without any jerk or the slightest personal danger, is placed on his feet in the middle of the room, where, at the option of the possessor, a cold bath can be placed, if he is at all disposed, to ensure being rendered rapidly wide awake. (129)

LIST OF SOURCES

1–5. *Punch.*

6. *Twenty Shillings in the Pound,* by W. Macqueen Pope. (Hutchinson.)

7. *Period Piece—a Cambridge Childhood,* by Gwen Raverat. (Faber & Faber.)

9. *Eli of the Downs,* by C. M. A. Peake.

10. *Letters of Charles Dickens to the Baroness Burdett-Coutts,* edited by Charles C. Osborne. (John Murray.)

11. *Hospitable England in the Seventies,* by Richard Henry Dana.

12. *Mrs. Beeton's Book of Household Management.*

14. *Notes on England* (1872), by H. Taine.

15. Letter of the 1890's.

16. *Punch.*

17. *The Reign of Queen Victoria,* edited by T. H. Ward. (Smith Elder & Co.)

18. *Conditions in York in 1901*—a report on the results of an investigation conducted by Mr. B. S. Rowntree into the economic and social conditions of the wage-earning class in York.

19. *Canon Barnett, His Life, Work and Friends,* by his wife. (John Murray.)

20. *Conditions in York in 1901.* See 18.

21. *The Nineteenth Century and After,* Vol. XLIX, January–June, 1901.

22. *Hospitable England in the Seventies,* See 11.

24. *Canon Barnett.* See 19.

25. *Punch.*

26. Report of a Commission of 1861.

27. The British Almanac of the Society for the Diffusion of Useful Knowledge, for the Year of Our Lord, 1871.

28. The School Log-Book of Miss Annie Pink.

29. The School Manager's Series of Reading Books adapted to the requirements of the New Code.

30. *Canon Barnett.* See 19.

31. *The Reign of Queen Victoria.* See 17.

32–3. *Punch.*

34. Letter written by Marianne Thornton to Miss Louisa Inglis, quoted in, *Marianne Thornton,* by E. M. Forster. (Arnold.)

35. *Canon Barnett.* See 19.

36. *The Labour Annual,* 1899.

37. *Punch.*

38. Report of a Committee inquiring into the running of Public Houses, 1854.

39. *Canon Barnett.* See 19.

40–1. *Twenty Shillings in the Pound.* See 6.

44–5. *The Reign of Queen Victoria.* See 17.

46–7. *Baily's Magazine of Sports,* 1868.

48. *Sporting Times,* 1882.

49. *British Almanac*, 1871. See 27.
50. *Mary Gladstone, her diaries and letters*, edited by Lucy Masterman. (Methuen.)
51. *Punch*.
52. *Illustrated London News*, May 1, 1877.
53. A letter written in 1877.
54. *Period Piece*. See 7.
55. *Twenty Shillings in the Pound*. See 6.
56–7. *Mary Gladstone, her diaries and letters*. See 50.
58. *A Frenchman sees the English in the Fifties*, adapted from the French of Francis Wey by Valerie Pirie. (Sidgwick & Jackson.)
59. *Punch*.
60. *The Greville Memoirs*, edited by Henry Reeve. (Longmans, Green.)
62. *Period Piece*. See 7.
63. *The British Almanac*, 1871. See 27.
64. Letter written by Marianne Thornton in 1882, quoted in *Marianne Thornton*, by E. M. Forster. (Arnold.)
66. *The Royal Kalendar and Court and City Register*. (R. and A. Suttaby.)
67. Queen Victoria's *Journal*.
68, 71. *Punch*.
72–3. *Letters of Charles Dickens to the Baroness Burdett-Coutts*. See 10.
74. *Notes on England*, by H. Taine.
75. *In Darkest England and the Way Out*, by General Booth.
76. *Punch*.
77. *The British Almanac*, 1871. See 27.
78–80. Queen Victoria's *Journal*.
81. *The Diaries of Lady Charlotte Guest*, edited by the Earl of Bessborough.
83. *Punch*.
84. Evidence given before a Royal Commission of 1864.
85–7. *Punch*.
88–9. *Canon Barnett*. See 19.
90. *The Reign of Queen Victoria*. See 17.
91. *Punch*.
92. *The Greville Memoirs*. See 60.
93–4. Parliamentary Papers, 1864 and 1863.
95. *The Criminal Prisons of London*, by Henry Mayhew and J. Binny. (Griffin, 1862.)
96. Letter from Charles Dickens in *The Times*, November 14, 1849.
97. *Mary Gladstone*. See 50.
98. The Royal Kalendar and Court and City Register. See 66.
99. *The Reign of Queen Victoria*. See 17.
100–1. *Mary Gladstone*. See 50.
102. *The County Councillor's Guide: a handbook to the Local Government Act, 1888*, edited by Henry Hobhouse and E. L. Fanshawe. (Maxwell & Son.)
103. *Fifty-one Years of Victorian Life*, by the Dowager Countess of Jersey. (John Murray.)
104. *The Greville Memoirs*. See 60.

105.] An article on Religion and the Churches in the Reign of Queen
107.] Victoria, by the Rev. Edwin Hatch, D.D.
106. *Canon Barnett.* See 19.
108. *The Reign of Queen Victoria.* See 17.
109. *Punch.*
110. *The Reign of Queen Victoria.* See 17.
111. *Fifty-one Years of Victorian Life.* See 103.
112. The Records of the New Zealand Co. in the Turnbull Library, Wellington, New Zealand.
113. *The Reign of Queen Victoria.* See 17.
114. *The Times*, December 9, 1859.
115. An article on India in Queen Victoria's Reign, by Sir Henry Maine.
116. *Western Africa, Its History, Conditions and Prospects*, by J. Leighton Wilson. (London, 1856.)
117. *Letters of Charles Dickens to the Baroness Burdett-Coutts.* See 10.
118. *Canon Barnett.* See 19.
119. *Punch.*
120. *The Reign of Queen Victoria.* See 17.
121. Anthony Trollope, 1872.
122. *The War*, by W. H. Russell. (Routledge, 1855.)
123. *Recollections of Lady Georgiana Peel*, compiled by her daughter Ethel Peel. (John Lane.)
124. An article on the Army in the reign of Queen Victoria, by General Viscount Wolseley, G.C.B.
125. *Records of the Fleet*, by Lord Fisher.
126. An article on the Navy in the reign of Queen Victoria, by Lord Brassey.
127. *Modern Painters*, Vol. 3, by John Ruskin. (Routledge, 1856.)
128. *The Nineteenth Century and After*, Vol. XLIX, January–June 1901.
129. An advertisement from *The Expositor*.

GEORGE ALLEN & UNWIN LTD
London: 40 Museum Street, W.C.1

Auckland: 24 Wyndham Street
Sydney, N.S.W.: Bradbury House, 55 York Street
Cape Town: 109 Long Street
Bombay: 15 Graham Road, Ballard Estate, Bombay 1
Calcutta: 17 Chittaranjan Avenue, Calcutta 13
New Delhi: 13—14 Ajmeri Gate Extension, New Delhi 1
Karachi: Meherson's Estate, Wood Street, Karachi 2
Mexico: Villalongin 32–10, Piso, Mexico 5, D.F.
Toronto: 91 Wellington Street West
São Paulo: Avenida 9 de Julho 1138–Ap. 51
Buenos Aires: Escritorio 454–459, Florida 165
Singapore: 36c Princep Street, Singapore 7
Hong Kong: 1/12 Mirador Mansions, Kowloon